Cowboys Are Partly Human

Little Girl: "Mommie, do cowboys eat grass?"
Mother: "No, dear, they're partly human."

Maverick Books

COWBOYS ARE PARTLY HUMAN

John R. Erickson

Illustrations by Gerald L. Holmes

This one is lovingly dedicated to
Kris Erickson

Contents

Cow Dogs

Back around 1973 the cowboy population of this country reached an all-time high. There was money in cattle at that time and the entrance requirements were not too high. To become a cowboy back then, a man had to invest in one bale of hay and two cow dogs, which were to be displayed in the back of a pickup, which was to be parked in front of the coffee shop several hours each day.

The market wreck of 1974–75 took a lot of cowboys out of the business, leaving only those of us who were not qualified for more respectable forms of employment. Also, our professional standards may be higher today than they used to be. To be a cowboy in 1979, you not only have to own a bale of hay and two cow dogs, but also a pair of Tony Lamas and three nylon ropes. And you must be qualified either in Skoal or Copenhagen. That gets a lot of them right there.

Cowboy numbers are down, and so is the cow dog population. What ever happened to all those cow dogs that used to sit in the backs of the pickups and growl at everyone who went into the coffee shop? Maybe the finance companies took them back. Maybe, during the lean years, they ended up in the deep freeze. I don't know where they went, but you don't see as many of them today as you did back in the good ole days.

Cow dogs are a lot like saddle horses. Every one you see has good breeding and is worth a tub of money. I wouldn't be surprised if some of the best dogs in this area come out of Three Bars breeding. If you believe what you hear, two thirds of the horses and half the fenceposts around here are Three Bars bred, so it would only be natural if most of the dogs were too.

But whatever the breeding, a cow dog in the back of a pickup is just another mutt. It's when he goes to work that he really proves himself. I've worked around a few well-bred cow dogs and I've seen what they can do. It's really impressive.

For instance, I've never known a breed of dogs that could pee on more tires. Leland, our neighbor to the west, has a cow dog that can wipe out all the tires on a pickup and stock trailer and still come back and bark at you before you reach the front porch. What a dog.

Out in the pasture, a good cow dog can fall in behind a north-bound herd of cows and have them going south in just a matter of minutes. Cows, stupid brutes that they are, can't seem to distinguish a high-bred cow dog from a prowling coyote and are given to displays of temper when either appears.

I once thought that cow dogs chased cattle. Now I know it's the other way around.

A good cow dog is intelligent enough to know where the gate is and what it's used for, and then to stand in the middle of it and bark.

A good cow dog won't chase a jackrabbit away from the herd. He will chase him right through the middle.

A good cow dog has been trained to respond to the command, "Damnit, go home!" On hearing this command, the dog will drop his head, tuck his tail, and remain exactly where he is.

If the cowboys happen to get the herd gathered and into a corral, a good dog will pitch right in and try to make a hand.

Last week a friend of mine related the following experience, which demonstrates the heroic qualities you look for in a good cow dog.

The cattle were gathered and penned and the crew was trying to move the herd into a smaller pen. The dog jumped right in to help. He tormented a horned cow until she spun around and went after him. This was an experienced cur, and he knew just how to respond to a fighting cow.

He ran and took refuge between the legs of the nearest

G.L.Holmes

cowboy, who happened to be my friend. My friend looked up just in time to see what it was that knocked him down. The cow rolled him, hit him again, and blew snot all over him before she finally let him up.

He has been hobbling around for two weeks now, but he feels that everything turned out pretty well. He didn't get any broken bones, but most important, the dog escaped injury.

After relating this experience, my friend added a gem of philosophy which puts the whole matter of cow dogs in its proper perspective:

"What every ranchhand needs is three stud horses, a cow dog, and a big ringworm."

Shakespeare couldn't have said it better.

The Cowboy's Rope

The lariat rope is one of the most practical pieces of equipment ever devised. It has no moving parts, never needs grease or oil, and there are no batteries to replace or wires to short out. It never overheats in the summer or fails to start in the winter. And if left out in the rain, it won't rust.

There seems to be no end to the chores it can perform. It's a portable calf-catcher and doctoring chute. Or, used in combination with a stout horse and a stock trailer, it becomes a cow loader-upper in remote pastures where such civilized luxuries as corrals don't exist.

If you're driving a lazy bull, you can coax him along by slapping him on the rump with your rope. If you're about to be attacked by a snuffy cow, you can pop her on the nose with the honda; this will either frighten her away or provoke her into crawling up into the saddle with you.

A lariat is still the best rattlesnake killer on the market, and under range conditions it's not a bad calf-puller. If you get wet, you can hang out your laundry on it. If you come to a stiff gate, you can throw a loop over the corner post and gate stick, dally up short, and back your horse. One way or another, the gate will open, sometimes with the corner post still attached.

5

If your horse is bad about breaking reins and headstalls, a loop around his neck and a half-hitch over his nose makes a dandy halter. If he goes back on it, the nose loop will tighten down and he will be marked by a ring around his snoot.

The nylon is also an indispensable tool in the treatment of hardware stomach in cattle. Does that sound far-fetched? Not at all. In this type of case, a nylon rope is more important to the cowboy-vet than all the wonder drugs of modern science. Here is the prescription from one who has used it several times.

First, keep the cow up in the lot for two or three weeks. Second, pour about fifty dollars' worth of medicine in her and about twenty dollars' worth of feed. Third, when she dies drop your nylon on her hocks and drag her over the hill. The medicine may fail you, but the rope will work every time.

In the Panhandle we also use the nylon for brush control. This method is quite a bit less expensive than spraying and chaining and all those other remedies.

Along about three o'clock in the afternoon, the cowboys will start taking down their ropes. They'll drop their loops over the nearest sagebrush, dally up, and jerk them out by the roots. There is no pollution or environmental damage in this method, but when the nylon snaps back and a green horse is popped on the butt by a sagebrush plant, bad things can happen.

If the nylon rope is an indispensable tool and piece of equipment, it is also the cowboy's most important play toy. Any discussion of ropers and roping which didn't touch on the whimsical side of roping would certainly be in error.

On a long cattle drive, when you find yourself back on the drag, nodding off to sleep and choking on the dust, you just naturally reach for your nylon. You rope every third fence post. You rope sagebrush and soapweed. You heel the baby calves. Then you heel a fat old cow. When you get double

hocks, you think, "Why not?" and you dally up and take out the slack.

But at the last moment, she pulls one foot out, the noose draws tight on her left hock, and you spend the next half hour trying to fish your rope off—without letting the boss see what you've done. It's good clean fun and it keeps the help occupied.

And then there are the cold, crisp mornings when the horses are frisky and the Devil is riding on the crew. For some reason, the Devil seems to prefer those crisp October mornings. His naughty ideas just seem to work better in cool weather.

The morning air is clean and quiet as the crew rides toward the back side of the pasture. Then all at once, a nylon is stretched between two horses. Two cowboys ride forward, slip the rope under the tail of old Blood and Guts, and yell, "Watch the rope! Watch the rope!" Old Blood and Guts snorts, swallows his head, and blows his sleepy rider right out of the stirrups.

The Devil is pleased. The crew is entertained. The unfortunate cowboy mutters that that's a helluva way to start the morning.

Before we end this discussion of rope-as-toy, we should consider the cowboy's irresistible impulse to dab his loop on uncommon targets—that is, roping critters that he shouldn't orta rope.

My friend Henry, up in Texas County, Oklahoma, jumped a coyote one day and was overwhelmed by a sudden desire to put a head loop on it. He kicked his horse into overdrive and gave chase. He was up in the stirrups and ready to throw, and then it happened.

When his horse stopped rolling, old Henry had several busted ribs and a cigar plastered all over his face.

And then there was Mark in Beaver County, who just couldn't ride past that badger down on the meadow. He latched on, dallied up, and rode off. He soon learned two important lessons about badgers. First, you can't drag them to death, and second, they won't give your rope back when you're through playing. Every time Mark stopped, the badger came after his horse. He rode in a circle for fifteen minutes, yelling for help. Finally Virgil came to his rescue and knocked the badger in the head with a fence post.

G.L. Holmes

Hobart tells the story about a man he knew in his youth. This Oklahoma cowboy rode up on a bobcat one day many years ago. He reached and roped and dallied and rode, but not fast enough. The bobcat rode off with him. The horse got his guts raked out and had to be shot, and the cowboy carried big ugly scars on his back the rest of his life.

I've heard a few yarns about cowboys who couldn't resist roping deer, and these stories never had happy endings. Deer may be shy creatures and have pretty brown eyes, but when roped, they're tough, and what a deer can do to a horse isn't even funny. Where deer are concerned, you can save yourself a lot of grief by leaving your rope coiled up and tied to the saddle.

When you think about it, that's not bad advice, whether you're dealing with deer or badgers or cattle. A catch rope can get you into trouble faster than a whiskey bottle or a painted woman.

But who can resist the temptation? My four year old boy is already trying to rope cats and dogs and peafowls. If an elephant ever walked through the place, I suppose he'd try to rope it too. And what's worse, I'd probably be right behind him, ready to reach for the heels.

Which just goes to prove that if you took the whiskers and snuff away from a cowboy, you'd find an unusually large four year old kid. But if you took his rope away, there would be nothing left but a common man.

That's one nice thing about this business. We may be broke and arthritic, but as long as we've got a rope in our hands, we'll never be common.

Feeding Hay

Last night I peeled off my long-john underwear for the first time in three days and found alfalfa leaves in my navel.

The oldtimers talk about the signs of a hard winter: the length of hair on the horses and cattle, the height of a prairie dog mound, and so forth. I took the alfalfa leaves in my navel as an unmistakable sign that winter has struck.

There are other signs as well, including snow on the ground and six inches of ice on the stock tank in the corral. And several cowboys in the neighborhood have started scanning the Help Wanted ads in the *Livestock Weekly* for ranch jobs in Jamaica and the Bahamas.

We started feeding hay right after Christmas. Luckily, Santa Claus brought me a new pair of elk hide gloves. My only complaint is that he purchased them in Beaver and charged them to me. I'm not old enough to remember a time when gloves were ever cheap, but it seems to me they have gotten outrageously high in the last few years. Are we importing our elk from the OPEC nations?

For ten bucks, you can buy a "cheap" pair of gloves that were made to fit someone whose thumb grows out of the top of his wrist and whose little finger is as long as a carrot. Some day I would like to meet the guy they used as a model for these gloves.

For fifteen bucks, you can buy a pair that fit, but which develop a hole in the end of the middle finger a week after you use them on alfalfa hay.

I'm sure that somewhere in this great land of ours, there is a pair of gloves that are hay-proof, but you'd probably have to hock your saddle to make a down payment. If cowboys ever get a union contract, let's forget the pension fund and go for a generous glove allowance.

On the whole, feeding hay in the winter is rather pleasant work, but I have a few complaints. I would like to speak to the man who baled that alfalfa in the stack south of the house. Was he angry that day? Did he hate hired hands? Was he trying to squeeze the whole cutting into a dozen bales?

They have the texture of brick. They are four feet long and weigh a hundred pounds apiece. I call them "chiropractor bales" for obvious reasons. I have called them other things, but such language is unprintable.

What annoys me most about these bales is that, while they weigh a hundred pounds apiece, the wires will only hold ninety-nine pounds. This means that after grunting and hefting the bale up to your knees, staggering into the back of the pickup and stumbling through the snarl of yesterday's baling wire, taking a deep breath of cold air and putting all your strength into throwing it up on the fourth tier—the wires snap in unison and the bale explodes in mid-air.

You usually get two or three pounds of it in your face and down your neck. I believe this accounts for the alfalfa leaves in my navel. Also the stems and sandburrs in my long underwear, which keep me squirming and scratching throughout the day.

Yes, I would like to speak to the man who baled that alfalfa. I would also like to give him my feed run for a week. He

who bales it should feed it. If he did, I'll bet he could figure out a way of cutting that baler down to sixty pounds.

Feeding in the snow has a few advantages over feeding in open weather. For one thing, the cattle aren't so scattered over the pasture. They stay pretty close to the feed ground. They come right to the pickup—and start eating before you string out the hay. Occasionally, this leads to a phenomenon known as the "self-unloading load."

The cowboy gets first warning of this when three bales of hay come crashing down on the cab. If he is snoozing, he usually awakens in an abrupt manner, popping his neck and damaging his knee on the steering column. This is often followed by profane oaths, as the hay slides down the windshield and amputates the radio antenna. (By mid-afternoon, it will be replaced by a stalk of baling wire, which will remain on the pickup until it is traded off.)

The animals who help the cowboy unload his hay are rarely popular. I carry a piece of windmill rod to express my feelings to them, and there is one horned cow in the east pasture who has been thrashed and speared so often that I fear it may affect her personality. I have also noticed that a frozen cow chip, well placed between the eyes, will discourage most cows from eating off the truck.

When the cows are all in, you climb on top of the hay (unless you've already deposited it on the ground in one great pile) and try to get a count. In a big pasture, this is a bit like counting leaves in a whirlwind. The cows mill and bawl. On your first count, you get 153. On your second count, you get 68. Writing the figures down in the palm of your glove, you add them together and divide by two. This yields the correct count: 110½.

Cowboy ingenuity will triumph over the most difficult of circumstances.

Having gotten your count, you walk through the herd and look the cattle over. Have you ever noticed what stupid expressions cattle wear on their faces when they are waiting for feed? You find such dull expressions in only a few other places in the world: in a college lecture hall and in church.

In the depths of January, you learn how well you culled the herd in October. You thought you did pretty well and had sent all the grandmas to town, but there are five Ace Reid Specials left in the herd that you will have to look at every day until spring.

How could you have missed them? They measure eighteen inches across the chops, three feet from horns to nose. Viewed from the side, they resemble an Arabian camel. Viewed from behind, they look lika a xylophone covered with a wet blanket. Last summer, you rode up on a cow out in the pasture that looked just like these. She had been dead for a week and a half.

Now you put the pickup in compound, hop out, and let her go. If you're lucky, you'll get the hay off before the pickup plunges over a cliff or buries itself in the river. Surely there is no funnier spectacle in the American West than a cowboy, bundled up like a robot, chasing his pickup across the pasture in four buckle overshoes.

If John Wayne ever did this in a movie, he would be laughed out of Hollywood. An outraged public would scream that no gen-u-wine cowboy would ever stoop to such silly behavior.

What the American public may not know is that gen-u-wine cowboys have to work for a living, and in the process they have to do a lot of things that are not only silly but derned inconvenient. One of those things is feeding hay in the winter.

Let's hope nobody ever makes an accurate movie about cowboys. I don't think our reputations could stand it.

Calving Heifers

A sense of humor might be defined as mankind's refusal to believe that things are as bad as they really are. In the day of Mark Twain, this was a common American attribute. In our day, ranchers and cowboys may be among the last of our race who have maintained their sense of humor.

They have done it against incredible odds. The odds in ranch work have always been incredible. The odds that anyone could be found who would actually *do* ranch work have always been incredible. Cowboys have maintained their sense of humor through courage, determination, and sheer stupidity. There should be some reward for this kind of human tenacity. If there is, we had better hope it awaits us in heaven, because there is little evidence of it here in Texas.

There should be something funny about calving out heifers. There should be something funny about calving out heifers. There should be something funny about calving out heifers.

I have been muttering this to myself for three weeks now as I have stumbled through the darkness, snow, and mud. I have always known that I was short on brains, but up until recently I had thought that the good Lord had worked out a fair trade, giving me someone else's sense of humor while giving my brains to another who was in a better position to use them. But my sense of humor has failed me of late. There is nothing funny about calving out heifers.

You breed your heifers to calve in March because history tells you that March will probably be warm and dry. Ha. Since you don't have a nice heated barn with running water and a friendly stove, and since you must perform your obstetrical chores on a windy hill, you try to protect yourself from the elements by employing the strategies of Planned Parenthood.

Oh, there were a few pretty days in March, perfect days for giving birth. And what did your heifers do on those days? They stood around eating, drinking, and staring at you with vapid eyes as you begged them to get it over with while the weather was nice. They were so ripe they could hardly walk, but somehow they managed to wait until the norther blew in. Then they went off like a box full of loaded mousetraps.

You bred them to a bull that had some Brahman in him, knowing that those small-hipped little jackrabbit calves would come flying out like watermelon seeds. You knew that because you had read it in the stock journals.

How many times had you read it? The subject of the article, a successful rancher, had said, "Naw, I'll tell you the truth. Since we brought in them Rhode Island Red bulls, we've thrown away our pulling chains. We bred three thousand heifers to them bulls last year and didn't pull a calf."

Crouched there in the alley, your boots sinking out of sight in the mud, you remember that statement. Your arms are bare to the shoulders, wet with disinfectant and turning blue in the wind. Your fingers are so numb they can hardly feel the pulling chains. You look to the sky and see the snowflakes swirling around your frozen ears.

You look at the heifer before you, at the two little hooves and tongue showing beneath her dirty tail. You insert your frozen hand into her body and rebuke her as she crushes it against her pelvis bone.

17

You jack the come-along, grunt, strain, and curse until the calf's head pops free. You discover the calf has hung in the hips. You reel out slack, get another bite with the cable, grunt, strain, and curse some more. The calf comes flying out and you go flying into the side of the barn.

The wet and slimy thing looks up at you as if to say, "Why?" And you glare back at him as if to say, "Hell if I know." And you begin to suspect that someone didn't tell the whole story about those Rhode Island Red bulls.

You will cancel all your subscriptions when you get back to the house.

Heifers are an outrage to human rationality. No one has ever explained why a heifer that is springing heavy in the pasture will suddenly lose all signs of pregnancy when she is brought to the house for closer observation.

No one has ever explained why the heifer you left in the pasture because she was a month away will calve that very night—in a blizzard.

No one has ever explained how the heifer you put up in the lot because she was as ripe as a bowl of jello and because all the signs said she was going to go off at any minute—how that heifer can go for another three weeks while you check her five times a day and carry her every bite of feed and every drop of water.

And no one has ever explained why it is that, when heifers have trouble in the pasture, they invariably get themselves halfway under a barbed wire fence.

I have said that there is nothing funny about calving out heifers. I want to change that. It is seven o'clock in the morning. There is just enough daylight now so that I can see the broomweeds bend double by the norther that blew in last night. I can make out a few snowflakes in the air. And I can see the prostrate form of an animal out in the heifer trap—one of the heifers I turned out last night because she was two weeks away.

I think I know what she is doing out there. I think she is halfway under the fence. I think I am banging my head against the typewriter. I think I hear a burst of laughter coming from my innards.

If so, then there must be something funny about calving out heifers.

Sweet Spring

"Sweet spring, full of sweet days and roses."
—George Herbert

Throughout the ages, poets have had pleasant things to say about the spring of the year. It's a time of fresh air, warm sunshine, and rebirth. As far as I know, nobody has ever asked a cowboy his opinion on the subject or inquired as to what springtime meant to him.

To start with, springtime in this part of the world ain't full of "sweet days." It's full of long days and short nights, and the only roses I've seen this year were on my rump. Saddle roses, you might say.

My roses started growing last Monday when another fellow and I rode a six section pasture looking for strays. We were ahorseback for about seven hours and didn't find the cattle. The roses burst into full bloom the following day when I helped the boys over on the Three Cross outfit shuffle cattle around. By seven o'clock that evening, my butt hurt so bad I was standing up in the stirrups to keep from injuring the flowers.

If you're a professional cowboy, you're supposed to be

thick-hided, tough, and immune to the little discomforts that afflict common folks. I thought I was until I found myself ahorseback on the first hot day of the year, wearing a new pair of undershorts that were a little bit stiff. If you ever want to grow some roses where the sun never shines, that's the way to do it.

I didn't expect to get much sympathy for a sore tail, and sure enough, I didn't. Jake thought it was very funny, though he admitted that every now and then he gets a few saddle roses too. My wife thought it was hilarious, especially when I humbled myself to ask where she kept the Diaperene and ate my supper sitting on a pillow. After the meal, I took my Diaperene and wounded pride and holed up in the back of the house.

I couldn't see the humor in it.

The next morning, all the cowboys in the neighborhood were scheduled to meet at seven o'clock on the south side of the river for a long day of moving and sorting cattle. I would be spending the entire day sitting on my injured part, which I did not think would be much fun.

A saddle gall on a cowhorse can knock him out of commission faster than a bum leg, and the same ought to be true of the man who rides him, except that horses receive more consideration and better treatment than cowboys do.

But I was lucky. We got rained out Wednesday morning and I didn't have to drape my wounded body over a saddle. My roses are fading, and by Friday I shall be ready for action.

So much for spring roses. Now let's take a closer look at what the poets call the sweet air of spring.

There is such a thing as sweet spring air. It has the odor of green grass, sagebrush, and wild grape blooms. I notice it every morning at five when I go down to feed the horses, and every evening at eight as I drag myself through the yard gate.

But I have noticed that, between dawn and dark, spring air is not sweet, and that it smells a great deal like horse sweat,

21

fresh-branded hair, and cow manure. I have tried to compose a poem about these fragrances, but so far I've failed.

I have a feeling that even Shakespeare would have trouble composing poetry in a branding pen. What would he say when he grabbed the hind leg of a struggling calf, sat down in a bed of sandburs, choked on a cloud of white smoke produced by a hot iron, and got himself blasted with green manure? I imagine that springtime smelled better on the Avon River in merry old England than on the Beaver River in the Great American Desert.

Another thing I've noticed about the spring air in this country is that it buzzes. That's right, it buzzes—with house flies, horse flies, horn flies, bot flies, blow flies. Also with gnats and clouds of starving mosquitoes.

It's very hard to appreciate the sweet air of spring when it's full of insects that are armed with ice picks and determined to drink your blood.

And then there are the miller moths, which have descended upon us this spring like a plague. Millers are everywhere. Pour yourself a cup of coffee in the early morning hours, set it down for a minute, and when you come back to it you'll find a miller inside, doing the back stroke.

The other morning down at the saddle room, I picked up my saddle blanket and a hundred and fifty-seven millers flew out. Two of them flew down my neck, another got trapped between my glasses and my eyeball, and another tried to walk into my ear.

When I'd loaded my horse in the trailer and started down the road, I hit a bump and another covey of millers came out of the heater vents. Smashing millers brings very little satisfaction. They make a mess on the windshield, and if you get too preoccupied with executing them, your chances of widening the next cattleguard up the road are vastly improved.

Another thing I've noticed about spring is that you never know which hat to wear. Before daylight, when you go down

22

to feed the horses, it's so chilly that you put on your old felt hat. After breakfast, when you go down to saddle up, it's so warm that you go back to the house and trade your felt hat for a straw. By the time you reach the pasture the wind is blowing so hard that you park your straw and pull on a cap. After lunch, when the rain starts, you wish you had your felt hat again.

It doesn't really matter which headgear you choose. Chances are, it will be wrong.

You have the same problem figuring out how many clothes you should wear. If you don't go prepared for the chill of early morning, then you freeze. If you take enough clothes to stay warm in the morning, then by noon you've shucked off four or five layers. You've got the slicker tied on behind the

G. L. Holmes

23

cantle and a jacket tied on top of that. You've got a vest tied to the saddle strings on the left side of the swell and a flannel shirt draped over the horn.

It's fun to watch a cowboy try to rope something when he's got his entire wardrobe tied to the saddle. His horse resembles a pack mule, and in the heat of the chase, clothes are flopping in all directions.

Building a loop, he finds his vest right in the middle of everything. Swinging the loop, he snags it on his slicker. When he finally gets off a shot, he jerks his slack and wraps his shirt into the dally. And when he sets his horse down, he discovers that he planted a fifty dollar jacket somewhere in the tamaracks.

So much for springtime, "full of sweet days and roses." If you're a cowboy, the days ain't so sweet and the roses ain't the kind you'd want to give to your sweetheart.

Three-Letter Words

I have read that the human race began to advance when our distant cousins started using three-letter words: why and how.

While the monkeys and apes were struggling with a six-letter word (banana), our ancestors directed their why's and how's to the world around them and tried to figure out what made everything tick. Eventually this led to the creation of philosophy, art, and science, the invention of baling wire, and other notable achievements.

We have left the monkeys far behind. Over several million years of evolution, they have figured out how to peal a banana and that's about it. Some people claim they invented television, but that's nothing a sensible monkey would want to brag about.

It makes an interesting theory, that the human race advanced because we asked why and how. If it's true, then cowboys must be among the most highly advanced of all humans, because we seem to be asking why all the time.

For instance, why do windmills break down in the hottest part of the summer, and usually on the very day when you want to get off the ranch and go someplace? I'm not imagining this. I've seen it happen over and over.

25

The windmill chugs along all winter and spring and never misses a stroke. Then comes July. The mercury boils out of the thermometer. You want to quit early and go into town for an ice cream social. After lunch, you drive around the pastures and check the water.

If you want to quit at five, you will find the busted mill at four. It's not pumping. All the cattle in the pasture have passed the word that this is a weak mill, and they've swarmed around it. The tank is down to mud, moss, and tadpoles. Cows are standing on their heads trying to get a drink, and bawling.

Instead of eating home-made ice cream that evening, you haul water until ten o'clock and spend the next day re-leathering the top and bottom checks.

Now I ask you: How does a windmill know that it's July and that you wanted to go to town?

Here's another one that's puzzled me for years. Why is it that a baby calf will always go to the wrong side of a corral gate? The gate is wide open. The cows file out in orderly fashion. Do the babies follow? No sir, they head straight for the wrong side of the gate, stick their noses in the corner, and blat for their mommies.

You have to climb off your horse, grab them by an ear and a tail, and throw them out the gate. If this happened once or twice a year, a guy wouldn't think anything about it. But it happens every time. Why?

And why is it that trailer lights will work fine around the barn, but when you get caught out at dark and need them, they quit? This doesn't just happen to me. I've passed cowboys on the highway and I've seen what their trailer lights look like.

At a distance on a dark night, a cowboy's rig is the strangest sight in the world. You can't tell what it is, whether it's a Christmas tree with blinking lights, a bicycle, or a couple of drunks walking around with flashlights. I would guess that several UFO sightings were nothing more than hard-working

G.L.Holmes

cowboys trying to make it back to the house before the cops picked them up for putting on a mobile light show.

Why is it that you can carry a slicker behind your saddle for three years and never take it down, but the one day you leave it at home, it rains snakes and pitchforks?

And why is it that at the very time your four-buckle overshoes have gone to rot and ruin, the monsoon season sets in? The corral becomes a big swamp, with feed stalks and horse biscuits floating around in stinking black water, and you end up wading through it, wearing bread wrappers over your new boots. It ain't fair.

Why do horses always find an open gate? As you let the gate down, you look back over your shoulder. Not a horse in sight. You'll be coming right back, so you take the path of least resistance and leave it down—just for a few minutes. You have gone fifty steps when you hear the thunder of hooves and see your saddlehorses pouring over the hill, bucking and kicking to celebrate their new freedom.

Where did those danged horses come from, and how did they know you left the gate down?

Why is it that livestock on open range will stand in the middle of the county road? They've got three or four sections of good grass, but they stand in the road. You'd think that, after a month or two, they'd starve to death, but they keep coming back.

They are most obnoxious at night. Staring into the glare of headlights, they seem oblivious to profanity and blasts from a horn. If they do happen to break into a run, it is invariably down the road, not out into the pasture. Leland's cows, which live in the road between here and the highway, are the world's worst. I've never hit one, but I've moved them from one end of the pasture to the other on many occasions.

Why do these things happen to good, decent, law-abiding cowboys? I don't suppose we'll ever know. The human race has made tremendous advances since the days when our ancestors mingled with the apes, yet the lot of the common cowboy has remained about the same as it was a hundred years ago.

A windmill, a horse, a calf, a cow brute, or the Panhandle weather can still make a monkey out of him, and make it look pretty derned easy.

Good Help

We've all heard the complaint that you just can't find help any more. You hear it everywhere you go these days, especially on ranches. Nobody wants to do the dirty hard jobs on a ranch, they say.

I don't want to do them either. For years now I've been looking for the clean, easy jobs on a ranch. I just can't find any. I'm beginning to suspect that they don't exist.

But anyone who says that you can't find help to do the dirty jobs on a ranch is wrong. You can, and sometimes you can find more help than you ever wanted.

About a month ago I had to rope a heifer that had gone visiting in the neighbor's pasture, and load her into the stock trailer. When I left the neighbor's pasture, I was pulling a four-wheel stock trailer. When I arrived at the heifer pasture, it had become a three-wheel trailer.

I found the wheel, but the axle and hub were beyond repair. We ordered a new heavy-duty axle and hubs. The delivery time, we were told, would be two or three days.

Four weeks later, we still had no axle and hubs. Oklahoma City had back-ordered to Dallas, Dallas had back-ordered to Chicago, Chicago had back-ordered to Singapore or some such place. The freight had been put on a truck somewhere along the line, but that was the last we heard of it. It wasn't lost, it just wasn't found.

Finally we called around and located another axle in Woodward, and I spent a day on the road. But we got the parts.

Yesterday morning I had everything laid out: nuts, bolts, washers, hubs, bearings, seals, tools, and a big can of bearing grease. I was all set to stick her back together. This was your typical dirty ranch job, but I didn't mind it. And I didn't really want any help.

But along came Scottie, age five, with little Ashley, our past-yearling daughter, toddling along behind him. Both were smiling and both wanted to help.

"Now kids," I said, "I don't mind having you up here, but don't touch anything." Scottie nodded. Ashley just smiled. I worked and they watched.

Then I went to the shop for a piece of emory cloth. When I returned, Ashley was wearing the hub bolt on her middle finger and Scottie was hammering a cotter key into the ground.

"Here, here, you kids run along and play. Shoo." I confiscated the hub nut and the cotter key. Now, where was I? Inside bearing. I reached for the inside bearing. It was gone. Ashley was trying to eat it. "Ashley, you little snipe, give me that bearing."

I ran her down and removed it from her jaws. She squalled. I returned to the trailer. Now, where was I? Bearing grease. I reached for the can. It was gone, and so was Scottie. I found them both on the other side of the trailer.

"Scottie, please don't put grasshoppers into the grease."

He gave me a disgusted look. "Daddy, he needs grease."

"Uh huh. Well, we'll grease him some other time. Right now let's see if we can get daddy's trailer put back together."

I returned to my work. Now, the inside bearing. It had

vanished again. Ashley was peeking around a big cottonwood tree, grinning at me. In her smile there were no teeth, only steel rollers.

"Ashley!"

Finally, I got the bearing packed and slipped onto the spindle. Scottie watched the procedure. He dipped out a handful of grease and began packing a socket wrench. I bellowed and ordered him to clean up his mess.

While my head was turned, Ashley scooped up a box-end wrench and a pair of pliers. When I caught up with her, she was trying to overhaul the cat.

Scottie was greasing the outside bearing and his tennis

G.L. Holmes

shoe and wiping the excess grease on his pants. I explained to him about mommies and grease, and that greasy pants had been linked to spankings.

By this time Ashley had walked off with a screwdriver and was trying to unscrew the cat's tail. That was enough. I banished them both to the yard and finished the work in peace.

Who says it's hard to find help for the dirty jobs around a ranch? In my case, it's entirely too easy. All I have to do is uncork a can of grease and in a matter of minutes I've got enough help to turn any half-hour job into three hours of chaos.

Cowboys and Equipment

Cowboys belong to a profession that requires the daily use of many types of equipment. Some of these devices make our life and work easier, while others should but don't.

For what it's worth, let us compile a list of the five best and five worst inventions of all time, a kind of Hall of Fame and Hall of Shame of ranch contraptions.

We'll start with the Hall of Fame. First place goes to a device with no moving parts. It is the one piece of equipment that no red-blooded American cowboy could do without. He carries it in his pickup and in his saddlebags, and uses it to repair fences, headstalls, gates, barn doors, and all manner of equipment from shovel handles to Diesel tractors.

Deprived of this device for thirty days, the American cattle industry would fall apart and cease to function.

Of course I'm talking about baling wire. I don't suppose anyone knows who invented baling wire, but someone in the cattle business should do some research on the subject and place a monument over the man's grave.

The next invention in the Hall of Fame should be the stock trailer. This device has vastly increased the mobility of the cowboy and has made easier such jobs as shifting cattle from one pasture to another, bringing heavy heifers in to the house, and moving furniture.

But to the ordinary cowboy, the most appreciated feature of the stock trailer is that, at the end of a long hot roundup day, it is there to transport a tired man and a tired horse back to the house. On that kind of day, when your mouth is dry, your rump sore, and your eyes full of dust; when you've already spent seven or eight hours in the saddle; when all you want in the world is a bath, a beer and a bed—the old stock trailer begins to look like a chariot sent from heaven.

And then we must mention vice-grip pliers in our list of inventions. Vice-grips hold the windmill rod in place while you're figuring the stroke. They hold stubborn bolts while you crank on the nut with a ratchet. They make fine welding clamps until you burn them up, and then you have to buy another pair to carry in your tool box and invent a few choice lies to cast the blame on someone else. And how did we ever change out windmill fan sections before we had vice-grips to clamp down on the other end so we could line up the holes with a screwdriver? Vice-grips have earned a place of honor in our Hall of Fame.

Any cowboy who has had the misfortune of being jerked off his horse and put on a haying crew should appreciate the next invention: the pop-up bale loader that fits on the side of a truck. Now, it could be argued that any device relating to hay is the creation of the devil and should not be given a place of honor. There is something to this, but we should remember the way trucks and wagons used to be loaded: heave-ho, stair-step, grunt, sweat, and swear. If we must have baled hay, then let us pause and give thanks for the pop-up bale loader. Life could be worse without it.

And finally, in our list of distinguished equipment and inventions, we must mention a substance which has revolutionized the cattle industry in just a few years: snuff.

If the federal government ever removed snuff from the

market, it would take two battle divisions of Marines to restore peace in the American Southwest. The most important ingredients in a modern spring branding are vaccine, fuel for the branding fire, and snuff. Snuff has changed the face of the American West. Now, under every third or fourth sagebrush, you find an empty Copenhagen can. It has also changed the face of the American cowboy by extending his lower lip anywhere from a quarter inch to a full inch and a half.

And snuff has changed his appearance in still other ways. Fifty years ago, the cowboy was the man in the chaps, spurs, and big felt hat. Today, he is the fellow with a Dixie cup in his hand and the little white ring on the hip pocket of his jeans.

Now we come to the Hall of Shame, a listing of inventions which never should have been invented and which have brought misery and woe to cow chasers all across the land.

My first nomination for this list is the posthole digger, not because it doesn't work, but because it works too well. You can't break a pair of steel-handled posthole diggers. Try to wear them out and you'll be in your grave long before they ever see a junkyard.

Posthole diggers have caused more blisters and inspired more profanity than any device known to man. When the fellow who invented this demonic tool went to apply for a patent, he should have been marched outside and shot. I can think of only one kind remark to say about the posthole digger. If we didn't have the PhD, we might be using something even worse.

Next on my list of worthless equipment is the two-minute hotshot. The two-minute hotshot can be bought in almost any stockman's supply store for around fifteen or twenty bucks. It works great in the store. You can hang it on a nail in the barn and leave it for six months and it will still work.

But on shipping day, when you have to load a set of calves into compartments of a pot-bellied truck; when you have to get that truck on the road; when the calves stop in the alley and turn around in the chute; when you can almost feel them shrinking—in short, at the very moment when you really need a good hotshot, it works for two minutes and quits. You bang it in the palm of your hand and get another buzz or two. Then you lose your temper and bang it on a corral post, which cracks the plastic case and ruins it forever.

Show me a frustrated cowboy and I'll bet the price of a haircut that he's got three hotshots lying around in his barn, and that on shipping day he'll end up whamming the cattle with a piece of sucker rod.

Next on my list of infamous inventions is the electronic ignition system, which now comes on most new pickups. At the very moment in history when most cowboys had just about figured out how to get along with points and condensers and old fashioned spark plug wires, some smart aleck designer in Detroit decided to "improve" the system.

The chief improvement, as far as I can tell, is that now when the pickup won't start, nobody, not even a trained mechanic, can figure out why. You can't file down the points any more or replace the condenser. They took away the good old-fashioned, honest spark plug wire and gave us something called a "lead," which is neither good nor honest, and whose primary feature seems to be that it carries a spark only when it feels like it.

As a result, one-third of all the new pickups in cow country are now equipped with V-8 engines which run on anywhere from five to seven cylinders most of the time.

If Detroit continues to improve our pickups, we'll all be ahorseback.

The next lousy invention we should consider is the $7.95 leather work glove. Now, to some of us, $7.95 is a lot of money to shell out for a pair of gloves, and we have reason for thinking that they ought to last for a while.

But they don't. Two days in a hay field and your fingernails are showing. Pull on a loose thread and all at once the

G.L. Holmes

thread is a foot long and your glove has fallen into two pieces. The annoying thing about these gloves is that you can never wear them out. They merely fall apart in the most critical areas, so that while the palm may be as good as new, the tips of three fingers are getting sunburned.

The manufacturer might claim that this kind of glove is made for "normal use"—which includes all forms of work for which you don't need gloves anyway. It is our misfortune to be involved in a business where "normal use" is often referred to as "loafing."

I have saved the most infuriating invention for last, and my vote for that honor goes to the high-lift jack. The high-lift is surely one of the best ideas to come along in fifty years, and probably the most disfunctional, cantankerous piece of equipment ever to ride in the back of a pickup.

I've often wondered if there's a high-lift in the country that works without a can of WD-40 and a pair of pliers. If so, I have never seen it. Those I've seen quit working after they had been rained on one time. By the time you need it, the mechanism is rusted and froze up, so that you have to bang, tap, coax, and pry to get it to work, while wondering when the handle will suddenly fly up and loosen your front teeth.

I know a man who claims to have found the secret for making his high-lift work. When he needs it, the first thing he does is to urinate on the lifting mechanism. That's no joke. He actually does that. I have never tried it so I can't say whether or not it improves the performance of the jack, but I can believe that, as an expression of outrage and frustration, it has something to offer.

I wonder if it would work on an electronic ignition system.

The Cowboy's Tractor

There is an ancient antagonism between stockmen and farmers. It goes back almost to the beginning of time. In the book of Genesis we find the first sign of trouble between the plowboys and the cowboys:

"Abel was a keeper of sheep, and Cain a tiller of the ground . . . Cain rose up against his brother Abel and slew him."

Abel got into a feud with his farmer-brother and lost. Modern stockmen can take some comfort in knowing that they lost the very first round. It goes a long way toward explaining what has happened ever since.

The hostility between plowboys and cowboys became a major theme in the history of the American West. From 1870 to 1885 the West belonged to the free-range cowboy. Then came railroads, bringing barbed wire and settlers and plows. The cowboys tried to drive off the settlers and farmers, but they didn't get the job done. The farmers came to stay, and stay they did.

They broke out the sod, planted crops, built churches, and invented 3.2 beer to keep the cowboys from doing outrageous things on Saturday night. And they replaced the Winchester with the grease gun.

Today the hostility between plowboys and cowboys is largely forgotten, or at least suppressed. Cowboys and farmers have learned to live together and their feuding is not as violent as it used to be.

One reason for this is that the distinctions between the two have been blurred in recent years. A lot of modern farmers run cattle on the side, and, like it or not, a lot of modern cowboys have been forced to do some farming on the side.

There is no funnier character in the modern West than the cowboy who finds himself playing the role of sod-buster. He is funny because farming violates his most sacred beliefs, and because he is so incompetent around machinery. A horseback, he may be an American hero, but mounted on a tractor he is doomed to play the part of a clown.

Let's take a closer look at his tractor. The cowboy-turned-farmer doesn't have enough country to justify the purchase of big expensive machinery. He has a little patch of wheat here, a dab of feed there, and a little field of hay grazer down on the creek bottom. It doesn't amount to much, and he can't afford to invest in high priced machinery.

He does his farming with used and cast-off equipment which some smart farmer traded in twenty or thirty years ago. His tractor is likely to be an old Case or a John Deere from the days when the green tractors lived up to the name Poppin' Johnny.

Today's farmer might keep one of these old tractors around as a toy for his children, but otherwise he wouldn't allow it on the place. What the farmer traded in twenty years ago is what the cowboy regards as his first-string tractor.

Over the years it's been cobbled on and patched up and it's as quirky as an old widow woman. The starter doesn't work so you have to hot-wire it with a screwdriver. No matter how many times you've done this, you can't keep from flinching when fire jumps across the end of the screwdriver. And when you flinch, you bark your hand on a piece of sharp metal and knock off a piece of hide the size of a postage stamp.

The screwdriver trick works fine unless the morning is too cool or there is too much moisture in the air. If the temperature is below fifty degrees or the humidity above fifty percent, you have to pull the tractor with a four-wheel drive pickup.

The exhaust pipe fell off ten years ago, so when you're going against the wind you're breathing a mixture of four parts diesel fumes, two parts dust, and one part oxygen. And to keep your ears from ringing all night long, you have to wear an ear protection device—chew up two pieces of a bolt sack and stuff the spit wads into your ears.

The fuel gauge doesn't work, so every three or four hours you run a shovel handle into the fuel tank to test the level. An experienced cowboy-farmer is so good at this that he can convert inches on a shovel handle into either hours or gallons, and do it all in his head.

The temperature gauge doesn't work either, which is a shame since a seal in the water pump has gone bad and it leaks water. You go to the field with two or three five-gallon cans of water. A full radiator will run three hours or until steam begins to hiss around the cap, whichever comes first. One of these days that water pump will have to be fixed.

Oh yes, and if you have to get out on the road and move to another field, you'll want to be careful because the brakes don't work very well. Actually, they don't work at all. If you're going down a hill, you may need to gear down. If you need to bring her to a whoa in a hurry to avoid a collision, you'll have to drop your plow into the ground. That's one reason the county road is a little rough in spots. It's been plowed a time or two.

But if you have to use the plow as a brake, you'll want to remember that the hydraulic lines are never hooked up the same way two times in a row. Cowboy-farmers can't seem to

42

remember which hose goes in which connection, and they're doing well to get them hooked up at all. So before you get on the road and need to use the emergency brake, you'd better test out the hydraulic lever a few times.

There are two levers, you know, a short one and a long one. Sometimes the plow works off the short one and sometimes it works off the long one. Sometimes the plow goes into the ground when you throw the lever forward, and sometimes it works just backward. And sometimes the blamed thing doesn't work either way. You'll get used to it after a while.

As for comfort, this tractor is guaranteed to keep you as warm as toast in the summer and as cool as frozen mackerel in the winter. If you run it much in the wintertime, you may want to buy a heater for it. Sears sells them for about fifteen bucks, and they're called long-john underwear.

One last word about this tractor. Don't wear your good clothes to the field. Anyone who gets within ten yards of this machine will get a new color and a new smell. It puts out a constant spray of old grease, new grease, hydraulic fluid, and diesel fuel. After you spend six hours around this tractor, you'll probably want to add a gallon of solvent to your bath water.

If your wife complains about your greasy clothes and doesn't know how to get them clean, she needs to try a new approach. Tell her to follow these simple directions:

Pick up the clothes with a long stick and carry them out to the back yard. Lay them down in the grass and turn on the water hose. Throw a match on the pile and run. After the clothes have burned for fifteen minutes, stir them around with the stick. You won't need the water unless the fire gets out of control.

44

Glasses

I was looking through a book the other day. It had some photographs of old-time cowboys, and some of cowboys on modern ranches.

Punchers have changed a lot in their appearance over the past fifty years, and the biggest difference, or at least the one I noticed, was that a lot of modern cowboys wear glasses.

It could be that the old-time punchers needed glasses but didn't know it or couldn't make it to the eye doctor. But if their eyes had been as bad as mine, I think they would have known it. The first time they went down to the barn before daylight and saddled up the milk cow, they would have suspected that something was wrong.

I couldn't get along without my glasses. They're the first thing I reach for in the morning and the last thing I take off at night. I doubt if I could hold a ranch job if I didn't have glasses. It's awful hard to read a brand when you can't find the cow.

But glasses can also be a pain in the neck. In the summertime when you sweat a lot around the face, your glasses start digging postholes in your nose. Sweat and salt get into the galls and make them worse. After a while you can't stand to wear them, but you can't see without them either, so what do you do?

They're almost as much of a nuisance in the winter when you're feeding cattle. When you get into a warm pickup after stringing out the feed, your glasses fog over and you've got to dig through five layers of clothes to find your T-shirt so that you can wipe them off.

And they're not worth much when you're out ahorseback in the rain either. I've been there a time or two. The rain starts pouring down. You reach back and untie the saddle strings and get a cramp in your side from twisting so far around. You

work out the cramp, while the water runs down the back of your neck. Finally you get your slicker untied and throw it around your shoulders.

And then your horse, who is six years old and has never seen a slicker before, boogers and bogs his head and starts doing the Panhandle two-step. You squint through your dripping glasses to see what he's going to do, and you can't seem to locate his head. You're as blind as a post.

If this happens when you're rounding up a big pasture, you stop worrying about finding cattle and start hunting cowboys. Since your vision through wet glasses is about what it would be if you were looking through wax paper, and since your vision without glasses is even worse, you begin to wonder how you're going to get out of here.

Glasses are also a nuisance when you're working around oil or grease, such as when you're up on a windmill tower, overhauling the head. Somehow you always manage to get a splash of oil on your glasses. You try to ignore it, but finally you can't stand it any more.

You take them off and wipe them on your shirt. But of course your hands are black with grease, and so is your shirt, and you end up smearing oil and grease over both lenses. You can't clean them with saliva because you're chewing tobacco.

So what do you do? Well, you find one little clear space at the top of each lens and you finish the job with your neck twisted, so that you can see out those little slots. It's frustrating, especially when you have sweat running into your eyes and flies crawling into your ears.

Last month I was trying to load a green horse into a stock trailer. He wouldn't load and I slapped him on the neck with the bridle reins. He threw up his head, caught me right square in the glasses, and sent them flying off my face. Before I could finish the loading lesson, I had to tie the horse, get down on my hands and knees, and feel around until I found my specs.

(Have you ever noticed that the time when a guy needs his glasses the most is when he's looking for his glasses?)

A couple of years ago I was out in the pasture riding a six year old mare that was about half-bronc. A locust flew up in front of her nose and she, weighing a mere twelve hundred pounds, was scared to death.

I had never entertained any illusions about winning the world on saddle broncs, though I'd always thought of myself as a pretty steady three-jump cowboy. But old Gypsy straightened me out on that. She blew me out of the stirrups on the first hop and threw me so high that the soles of my boots were reflecting the sunshine.

I landed face-first in a clump of sagebrush. When I looked up to see where Gypsy was going, my vision wasn't too clear, mainly because my glasses were sitting on my front teeth.

When a guy gets bedded down, he'd like to come away from it with a few hero marks, so that he can get some sympathy from his wife and children. All I got out of that deal was two scabs, one on each side of my nose, where my glasses pealed off the hide. Didn't get much sympathy.

Wrecks like that are hard on noses and they're hard on glasses too. My glasses have been hammered on and bashed up so many times that if I take them off and lay them on a table, they'll walk five steps before they fall.

Every now and then I'll get disgusted and try to fix them. When one lens sits up around your eyebrow and the other rubs on your cheekbone, you just have to get out the pliers and vice-grips. I usually get my glasses straightened out in the same way a cowboy-vet gets his sick cattle straightened out. When I get through with them, they need more than the usual band-aids and safety pins. They need a certified pipeline welder, or else a trip to the dump.

Cowboys were a lot better off back when they didn't wear glasses.

A Funny Way of Walking

If you read any books about the old West, you'll run into the observation that cowboys had a funny way of walking when they were on the ground, "like ducks out of water" or something along those lines.

The point the author is trying to make with this kind of observation is that the old punchers spent so much time in the saddle, they didn't know how to use their legs on dry land.

Could be, but I suspect there is more to it than that. I know a lot of contemporary cowboys who have a peculiar way of getting around, and I don't think it's because they have forgotten how to use their legs. There aren't many of us who ride that much any more.

I did some research on this last week, and I may have come up with the answer. I was out doctoring calves for pinkeye. I had captured three of the slippery little devils and was hot after number four. I was up in the stirrups and swinging my twine, when all at once the calf made a sharp right turn. My mare followed. I didn't.

The calf and the mare went south, and I kept on going east, lost a stirrup, and found myself reaching for things a good horseman ain't supposed to reach for—such as mane, saddlehorn, ears, reins, and sunbeams. I caught several sun-beams and one ear and managed to stay pretty much ahorse-back. Anyway, I didn't fall off, which would have hurt my pride. But I ended up hurting something else.

When I finally got the mare shut down, I knew I had changed the shape of my backbone, enough so that I had lost the urge to play with my rope. By the time I made it home, I was hurting. I left my rigging in the middle of the saddleroom floor, turned out the mare without grain, and crab-walked to the nearest bed.

G. L. Holmes

Now, if a writer had come along right then, he might have gotten pretty excited about the way I was walking, and might have mistaken me for one of the old-time saddle-warped cowboys. My step was sure 'nuff peculiar, and I may have even looked like a duck out of water, with bad corns and a double half-hitch in his spine.

This research project has given me some insight into the posture and walking habits of the old-time punchers, as well as those of the ranch and rodeo cowboys of the present day.

Hell yes they have a funny way of walking. When you've got a fallen hip, a lop-sided pelvis, a crooked backbone, and a cuttinghorse neck, you just naturally do things a little different. It's not that you've forgotten how to walk straight, it's just that you can't.

It's really amazing all the things you can't do when you've got your back on crooked. You can't walk, you can't lift, you can't sit, you can't spank the children, you can't hop into the pickup and go check the water and salt.

I couldn't even blow my nose for a week. I sneezed once on Saturday, and howled like a coyote for five minutes.

Of course there are a few things you can do. You can rope your toes with a pigging string. You can yell at the children when they come in and jump on the bed. You can walk to the bathroom and back, which about the third day seems pretty exciting.

And you can write a few letters: "Dear Jim and Mavis: Well, I ain't got much to say. Wrecked a horse and rearranged my backbone. How are yall doing? It sure hurts. We sure enjoyed seeing yall last month. I haven't had a chew of tobacco in three days. How are the kids? Dang I'm tired of this bed. I guess that's about all the news."

A couple of those letters and you run out of things to say.

You don't realize how many cowboys have back trouble until you bring up the subject of your own miseries, when you have to explain to someone why you crawled up the court-

51

house steps on your hands and knees, or why it took you half an hour to get out of the pickup.

Once you bring up the subject of back trouble, you hear lots of stories, and you discover that just about everyone in the neighborhood owns a bad back.

Stanley has had his back broken twice. Jake has a bum neck to go with his cracked ribs. Glen got his back stepped on by a bronc in Canadian last year, and I heard he was doing the crab-step for a while.

I don't know what Lloyd's trouble was, but I ran into him at the chiropractor's office last week. I was going out of the treatment room and he was going in. We both had our shirts off. He looked like a culled cowboy on his way to the rendering plant, and I probably looked that bad or worse.

Around here, if you want to see the neighbors, don't go to church or to the coffee shop. Go to the chiropractor's office. Sooner or later, they'll all come limping in.

A dog may be man's best friend, but I have an idea that a cowboy's best friend is the chiropractor. And that goes a long way toward explaining why cowboys have a funny way of walking.

Diary of a Steer

(Author's note: The following is taken from the diary of a black bald-faced steer, age eight months and weighing approximately 450 pounds. It deals with his experiences in the Texas Panhandle in the fall and winter of 1978.)

October 1, 1978: Spent most of the day in a cattle truck. I can't say much for the accommodations. It was crowded and noisy.

The fellow standing next to me was originally from Alabama, a tall thin guy with big horns and a long cowy head. He said we're going to the Texas Panhandle where the grass is always too short and the winters too long. He wanted to go back to Alabam and he bawled for three straight hours.

I got sick and tired of hearing him. Finally I told him, "Listen, pal, I've never seen Alabam but I've seen you, and I don't want to go there." That shut him up for a while.

Around five o'clock we unloaded at a set of corrals. I can't see much of the country from here, but it appears there's a little creek to the south and some cliffs and canyons up north. It's hot and dusty in this country, but I'm not complaining. We got some good grub tonight, sweet feed and alfalfa. The hay was put up too dry, but it's got a good flavor.

Next day: This place is all right. I didn't do anything today but eat and drink. Went from the feed bunk to the hay feeder. When this got boring, I wandered over to the water tank. This is the life. Even old Alabam filled up. He's not such a bad looking fellow after all. If you shortened his nose and tail by three feet, he'd pass for handsome.

We've got two cowboys taking care of us, John and Tom. Several times today they walked through the pen and looked us over. Just before sundown they brought in some more alfalfa hay. The food is excellent here, but these lots are awfully dusty. My allergies bothered me all day.

Next day: We had some trouble last night. One of the little guys came down with galloping pneumonia and died. John and Tom dragged him off with a pickup, and when they came back they went to work on us. They walked through the pen and when they found someone who looked thin or droopy, they cut him into the sick pen.

I was standing over by the water tank, minding my own business and chewing my cud. I got some dust up my nose and coughed, and the next thing I knew I was in the sick pen. They ran me into a chute, and while one of them stuck me in rump with needles, the other one poked three big white pills down my guzzle.

Next day: I spent the night in the sick pen with all the scrubs. This is outrageous. I've never received such shabby treatment in my life. They gave me more shots and pills today, even though I'm not sick.

All I did was cough at the wrong time. Who wouldn't cough in all this dust? Even John and Tom were coughing today. I wish I could get those two in the doctoring chute for about fifteen minutes.

Next day: Well, I got out of the sick pen today. I've learned one thing from this experience: don't cough when those two needle-happy cowboys are around.

Two days later: Yesterday the cowboys sorted us up into two bunches. My bunch was branded and turned out into the home pasture. We've got good grass and plenty of space. No more dust. I feel wonderful.

Next day: I don't feel so good today. Must be my allergies acting up.

Next day: I feel lousy. Maybe it's a sinus infection.

Next day: This ain't sinus. I'm sick. My nose is running and my ears are drooped so low I think they might fall off. I'm lying down in some sunflowers near the back side of the pasture. The cowboys rode by yesterday on horses. I had the feeling that they were looking for me, but they didn't see me.

Next day: They found me. They tried to drive me to the corrals but I wasn't in the mood for that. I wanted to sleep and be left alone. I went about a hundred yards and quit. When they tried to crowd me, I went after their horses. I guess I showed them a thing or two. They rode back to the house. I'm a pretty tough customer when I get mad. Gave those boys quite a scare. I doubt if they'll mess with me again.

Later that day: I underestimated the cowboys. They came back with a pickup and stock trailer. One of them stuck a rope on my neck and dragged me into the trailer with a big sorrel horse. If I'd been feeling better, I would have put up a better fight. Ordinarily, two cowboys are no match for me, and there isn't a horse alive that can push me around when I'm healthy. But I was feeling puny.

A week later: Spent a week in the sick pen. Every time I coughed or belched, one of those cowboys was coming at me with a needle or a pill. But I survived all their doctoring and I'm back in the home pasture.

I ran into Alabam today. The guy looks just as sorry as he did the day he got here. He's the worst looking steer in the bunch, but he hasn't spent a single day in the sick pen. That really hacks me off.

A week later: Lost my horns today. It happened so fast I didn't know it was coming. If I had, I might very well have destroyed the corrals in a display of brute strength. They ran me into a chute, put the squeeze to me, and then—crunch, no more horns. Sometimes I think Tom and John don't like steers.

Next day: Alabam lost his horns too and he bawled all night long. It hurt his pride. Two days ago, he was nothing but horns and backbone. Now he's nothing but backbone walking around on four legs.

Ten days later: The cowboys have left us alone since they knocked off our horns. Every day or two they'll ride past on horses and make us stand up and walk around. Those guys are so dumb they have to write their tally down in the palm of their hands. My cough is gone and I'm feeling much better.

Next day: Big doings today. The cowboys rounded up the home pasture. Me and Alabam gave them a run for their money. We got out in the lead and headed for the creek when they were trying to drive us into the corrals. Had a heck of a good time.

I learned something about Texas cowboys. They're pretty good hands ahorseback, but they're even better at cursing. They called us everything but nice before they got us gathered up.

When we finally gave up and went into the pens, the cowboys sorted off seventy-five of the best steers to go to wheat pasture. I, being the very handsomest of the bunch, was selected early. Somehow Alabam made the cut and he'll be going too.

Next day, November 10: We're on wheat pasture today. The country around here is as flat as a table, and looking in all directions I see nothing but luscious green wheat. I shall try to eat it all myself.

Next day: I tried to eat it all myself and came down with a bellyache. I puffed up like a toad and could hardly walk. The cowboys came by this morning and ran a rubber hose down my guzzle. That was undignified, but I feel much better now.

Four days later: Alabam and I got bored yesterday. We looked across the fence and decided that the wheat was better over there. He showed me how to hop over an electric fence, and off we went. We ate and walked, walked and ate. Never had so much fun. Old Alabam knows how to have a good time. Last night he suggested that we hit the road and head for the Deep South. He has lots of friends down there. That sounded like a good idea.

But this morning our cowboys friends showed up with a stock trailer and two horses. They wanted us to go back to the wheat field but we declined their invitation. We headed south in a dead run.

Must have made the cowboys mad because they cursed us and pulled down their ropes. They caught both of us and tied us to utility poles, then they went back to the trailer.

Tom was riding that same sorrel horse that stuck me in the trailer last summer. I decided he wasn't going to do it again. I braced all four feet and fought like a panther. Sometimes I'm amazed by my own strength. I wasn't going to let them put me in that trailer.

But you know what? They did. That sorrel son of a gun jerked me out of my tracks and threw me into the trailer so hard that I scabbed my nose on the front end. Then they did the same thing to Alabam. They gave him such a jerk that I think they lengthened his backbone by a full six inches.

I guess we'll stay home from now on.

A week later, November 24: Boy, it was hot today. Alabam said it was supposed to be cold in the Panhandle. He was wrong. It's been hot as blazes. Alabam is a nice fellow but he's a little short on brains.

Next day: It's snowing. The wind is blowing forty miles an

hour. I have a big icicle hanging on the end of my nose. Alabam cried all night long. He wants to go home. I want to go with him.

Last night, when the wind was blowing snow into our faces, he said something that I thought was kind of interesting. He was moaning about the cold and said something like, "It was a lot better in my former life."

I said, what do you mean, in your former life? And he said he'd been on this earth before, only then he wasn't a skinny steer. I said, well, what the heck were you? And he said, "A cowboy in the Texas Panhandle. I got sent to hell, but Satan said that was too good for me, so they sent me back to the Panhandle as a steer."

I don't know whether to believe him or not. But if he's right about this, then Tom and John are in for a rude surprise.

Yearling Man

People outside the cattle business probably don't know the difference between a yearling and a cow, and are perfectly content to leave it that way.

Neither are they aware of any differences between the several classes of cattlemen, such a the cow-calf operator and the yearling man.

At a distance the two types appear to be pretty much the same. They both wear boots, listen to the same radio station, and hold similar opinions on politics.

Either one will walk across the street to avoid speaking to a banker, spank his children for dreaming of a white Christmas, and complain when the weather is too dry or too wet—and it's always one or the other.

But on closer inspection, you can find some important differences between the cow-calf operator and the yearling man.

When a cow-calf man picks up a newspaper, he'll turn first to the sports page and work his way to the market quotations. A yearling man will go right to the futures section. He'll squint at the page for a minute, mutter an oath under his breath, and toss the paper in the trash can. For that reason, the yearling man is likely to be poorly informed on the football rankings.

If you're in a group of cattlemen, you can look at their hands and arms and pick out the yearling operators. The yearling man is the one with the tattoos on his left arm. If you look closer, you'll notice that they're not really tattoos.

That's his tally for the last three days. It started in the palm of his hand on Monday, worked up to his wrist on Tuesday, and by Wednesday it had moved up around his elbow.

You might also notice that when everyone else is washing up for lunch, the yearling man only washes his right hand. If he washed off his tally, he'd be in big trouble.

The yearling man also has a unique smell, and when he walks into a room you don't have to ask what he's been doing. If he smells like burned hair, he's receiving some new cattle and has been down at the branding pen. If he smells like Lysol and iodine, he's been castrating bulls.

If he just plain old stinks, then he's probably been fighting maggots all morning, and chances are that he's got half a can of pine tar on his clothes. If all the flies in the room drop dead when he enters, you know for sure that's what he's been doing.

Some people believe that yearling operators are individualists and loners, and in most cases they are. Anyone who goes around smelling like K-R-S smear will end up a rugged individualist.

You can check out a man's clothes and tell which end of the business he's in. If he clothes are clean or if they carry the faint odor of cottonseed meal, he's a cow-calf man for sure. If they're speckled with something that appears to be blue ink, he's a yearling man.

It's not ink. It's pinkeye medicine. The instructions on the bottle state very plainly that the medicine is supposed to go into the animal's eye, but a yearling man will end up wearing it on his pants, shirt, and boots. The skin around his fingernails is blue and so is the noose on his catch rope.

There are other signs that point to a yearling man, but you have to be sharp to catch these. If a guy walks past a hound dog, the kind with big droopy ears and sad eyes, and if he mumbles, "Fifteen cc's of Combiotic and two amino acid boluses," he's a yearling man.

If his mood darkens when he passes a rendering truck on the highway, he's a yearling man.

If he carries two ropes, three pigging strings, and a medicine bag on his saddle, he's a yearling man.

If the back end of his pickup looks like a junkyard, filled with electric fence posts, chargers, batteries, crumbs of alfalfa hay, and three hundred pounds of used baling wire, he's a yearling man.

If you attend a party and hear some jughead over in the corner talking about bloat and foot rot, he's bound to be a yearling man.

If you run into a guy who has red eyes and a runny nose, and who speaks in a hoarse whisper, he's probably a yearling operator who has spent the last week doctoring shipping fever in dusty corrals.

After about six days of this, the cattle look better and the cowboy looks worse. He appears to have come down with shipping fever himself.

It's fairly easy to spot the wife of a yearling operator. She's the little lady who knows how to use hay hooks and a hot shot. She buys her clothes only at the very best garage sales, and she takes the kids to vacation Bible school in a four-wheel drive pickup.

And it's easy to pick out the child of a yearling operator, provided the child is still young enough to give an honest answer to a question. If you ask this child, "Little boy, what does your daddy do?", he will answer, "He loses money."

Cowboy's Hell

I was raised a Southern Baptist, so I know a good deal more about Hell than I do about Paris, France.

We Baptists were interested in Hell because we wanted to know what the Methodists would be doing in the Sweet Bye-and-Bye. Our preachers made it out to be a pretty dismal place, and I never particularly wanted to go there, even for a visit.

So how do you explain that I dreamed about Hell last night? Beats me, unless it had something to do with that hot chow chow the neighbor's wife sent over. Boy, it was good over meat loaf, but I think she could have cut down on the gunpowder.

Now, I'd always pictured Hell as a big dark cave with a furnace at one end and a bunch of sweating sinners standing around with scoop shovels. Every now and then the Devil would come by with his pitchfork and stick somebody.

Well, it wasn't like that in my dream. Hell wasn't a cave. It was a big flat pasture with about five hundred sections under one fence. There wasn't a cloud on the horizon. It hadn't rained since the beginning of time, so you can imagine the grass was a little short.

In fact, there wasn't any grass, nothing but cockleburs, thistles, Mexican sandburs, and goatheads. The wind blew forty miles an hour, and the temperature stayed around 110. But worst of all, in Hell they didn't have chewing tobacco.

There wasn't any coal to shovel, just ranch work. The first five million years, I worked on the windmill crew. There were a thousand mills in Hell, and they were all broke down. Towers made of rotten wood. Ladders that fell apart in your hands. No platforms at all, just two pieces of angle iron to stand on.

All the fan bolts were loose, all the leathers worn out, all the rods as skinny as a pencil. And every place you put your hand, there was a yellowjacket nest.

On one mill, we spent ten thousand years trying to fish out the bottom check. Every time we got it to the top, it snagged on something and fell back into the hole. That's the most discouraging sound in the world, when the bottom check hits the water. Ten thousand years.

Then I got moved to the fencing crew. The Devil had a normal kind of fence—three rotten wires and posts that wouldn't hold a staple—and we spent, oh, a couple of centuries giving it a sharecropper's patch. That's when you connect rotten barbed wire to rotten posts with a piece of new baling wire, and stretch it up with your pliers.

But that wasn't good enough. As soon as we got the old fence patched, the Devil decided he wanted a new five-wire fence. Two hundred years rolling up wire, five hundred pulling posts with a high-lift jack and a chain.

Then they passed out the posthole diggers. No Ford tractors in Hell. Since they hadn't had any rain for several billion years, the ground was a little stiff. My first hole took five years to dig, and I quit counting after that.

The Devil had some dandy new posts to put in. Bodarks that weighed two hundred pounds apiece. If you worked it just right, you could drive a staple in less than a month. I'd sure like to meet the man who cut those posts.

G.L. Holmes

Well, we finished up in a couple of million years. Heck of a nice fence. You could have picked a tune on the wires, they were so tight. By this time the crew was all blistered up and gant as a bunch of blue racers, but proud.

The Devil came out to inspect. Said it was a heck of a nice fence and it was just a shame he'd forgotten to mention that the survey on the old fence was wrong and he wanted it all moved out two feet, because it sure was a nice fence.

Several million years later, I got fresh orders. Seems I'd been transferred to the septic-tank-cleaning-out crew, but just then my alarm clock went off, and this time I didn't go back to sleep. Half an hour later, Willie, my neighbor, drove up in his pickup. We'd planned to go fishing. It was Sunday morning.

"Can't go with you," I said. "I'm going to church." He gave me a funny look. "I dreamed about Hell last night, and it's got me scared."

He rolled a smoke and lit up before he said anything. "Did, huh. Was it worse than the Panhandle?"

"It was just more of the same, Willie, the Panhandle forever and ever."

He nodded, took one puff, and dropped the cigarette on the ground. "What time we leavin' for church?"

Holding Herd

On some modern ranches, cattle are driven to working pens and sorted through a gate by cowboys on the ground. Around here, we do most of our sorting in the old-fashion way.

The cattle are driven into a corner, and while part of the crew holds herd, two or three cowboys of the executive class do the cutting ahorseback.

Since I'm not a member of this elite group, during spring and fall roundup seasons I spend a good part of every day holding herd.

I suppose that some people would consider this menial labor, hot, dusty, and dull work that drags on for hours and hours. It is. There is always a certain percentage of cows and calves that won't pair up, and there are the inevitable conferences in the middle of the herd, when the cutters come together and debate whether this certain cow needs to go to town. It often goes like this:

"What do you think about that lineback cow there?"

"I'd say she's got cancer eye."

"It's not pinkeye?"

"Nope. Whole left side of her face is gone."

"Yeah, but she's still got the right side. Don't you reckon we can get one more calf out of her?"

"Probly. A guy sure don't want to ship any of his good cows."

Time tends to drag when you're holding herd, but I've noticed that ingenious cowboys have invented ways of amusing themselves.

I know one fellow who has a wart in the palm of his left hand. When things get dull, he brings out his pocket knife and starts picking at it. That wart has provided him with hours of good wholesome entertainment. I don't know what he'll do if it ever goes away.

Chewing and spitting are other forms of entertainment. I know a cowboy who lines up his horse's ears like the sights on a rifle and tries to spit between them. He's getting so good at this, he may run for Congress.

Another thing you can do outside of the herd is learn all the important information on the neighbors, such as whose pickup is in the shop, whose horse got a foot cut in some wire, whose mare was bred to a high-powered stud, whose cat had kittens, and which cowboys have been bucked off in the last two weeks. A guy needs to keep up with world affairs.

And then there is the usual run of practical jokes. In the heat of the day it's always fun to ride over and put the toe of your boot under the tail of the next man's horse. If he's drowsing, you can unhook his back cinch or slip the headstall over his horse's ears.

But these jokes get tiresome after a week or two, and a guy begins to dream up some new ones. I thought of a dandy this spring, but I haven't worked up the courage to pull it off yet. One of these days I'm going to slip a bullfrog into the water can. I think that one would be remembered.

Another thing you can do to pass the time is harass the cutters in the herd, and the best way to do this is to be "helpful." If they're cutting pairs, then you yell, "There's a

G.L. Holmes

pair," and point in the general direction of two hundred cows.

If they're cutting dries out of a herd of Hereford cows, then you call out, "Hey, that Hereford's dry, the one with the white face and the two ears."

The one I like the best is a bit more difficult. You have to wait until a calf is standing close to a bull, and then you use hand signals to tell the cutter that you've found a pair.

I wouldn't want to leave the impression that holding herd is all monkey business, or that a good professional cowboy spends all his time playing pranks. He doesn't. A true professional takes his work seriously. Instead of playing jokes on the other cowboys, he watches the cattle in front of him.

When a cow, bull, or baby calf comes to the edge of the herd, the experienced cowboy moves his horse and cuts the critter back in. When a yearling with a nice set of horns comes to the edge, a top hand will time his move just right so that the animal can escape.

Then he jams the gut hooks into his horse and begins the chase. Now, the chase is very important and it must be done just right. The cowboy must create the impression that he's trying to bring the yearling back, when in fact he's doing his derndest to drive him over the hill. This requires great skill and timing.

Once the critter has gone over the hill, the cowboy's face breaks into an evil grin. He unlatches the horn string, builds a loop in his nylon, and takes aim at that nice set of horns.

If he's a one-loop roper, he'll have the yearling back home in ten minutes. If he's a three-looper, it will take him somewhat longer. When he brings the critter back into the herd, four cowboys ride toward him at top speed, swinging heel loops. I've seen the time when the entire crew quit the herd and ran over each other trying to get a hock shot.

At some point during the day, the cowboy who roped the yearling will look up the boss and explain his action: "I sure hate to rope your cattle," he will say with a look of utter sincerity, "but that yearling just had it in his mind to quit the bunch."

The boss will nod and smile, perhaps remembering the days of his youth, and he will say something like this:

"Oh, that's all right. Them things happen when you're holding herd. I didn't mind you roping that first one, or even the second or third. But damn, son, that last steer almost made it back into the herd before you got a loop stuck on him."

Exposed in this way, the cowboy pulls his hat down and shuffles his feet. "Guess maybe I orta trade for a faster horse."

Skunks

We were very happy in our little house along the Beaver River. We had stayed warm through the coldest January on record. We had eaten well. We were all healthy. Our marriage was sound. Our two children were happy. But then . . .

My wife was the first to notice. It was around 9:30 at night. The children were in bed, the house was quiet at last, and we were enjoying a few minutes together. Suddenly Kris stopped talking. "Do you smell something?"

I thought we were in for a routine problem—the washing machine had caught fire, the house was burning, something routine.

I lifted my nose and tested the air. I smelled it, all right, and it wasn't smoke. It wasn't a sour diaper. It wasn't the Right Guard that Ashley had sprayed into the humidifier the day before. It wasn't burned toast.

It was a skunk.

Now, skunks were nothing new to us. We lived on a ranch and skunks were part of the scenery. Back in the fall, one had ventured into our garage at night. Foxie the Wonder Dog was occupying the garage at that time, after winning it from our three cats. No animal on the ranch dared enter her domain.

But the skunk did. Foxie bristled and growled a warning. The skunk ignored it and went on about its business. Foxie rose from her bed of rags and bared her fangs. The creature didn't leave. Foxie pounced on the skunk and was sprayed. She ran for her life, leaving the garage to the cats or anyone else who could stand it.

I didn't see this battle but reconstructed it from the evidence the following morning when I entered the garage to get a package of hamburger out of the deep freeze. I walked into the poisonous air and stopped in my tracks. I peered into the gloom, under old tables and lawn chairs, around boxes and stacks of magazines.

There he was, between me and the deep freeze, looking back at me with a pair of black, beady eyes. His tail was cocked and he was ready to fire.

Following the example of our cur, I backed out the door.

The skunk held the garage for two days. Foxie slept down in the hay lot and we ate beans and tuna fish. Then the skunk left and we were able to reclaim our supply of beef.

Skunks often came up into our yard at night. Sometimes we would see one eating out of the dog bowl, but usually we didn't see them. We smelled them. The odor would drift into the house, hang there for several hours, and then disappear. The next morning, Foxie would have that pitiful look of defeat on her face, and she would smell like a stale onion.

We were used to skunks. But as Kris and I sat there that night, we began to realize that this was going to be something special. The odor grew stronger and stronger. It was coming up through the floor. It was in the bedroom, the kitchen, the utility room.

It was everywhere, and it was rank. If you've never been close to a nervous skunk, you've missed one of the most appalling smells on God's earth. It is nauseating and over-powering. It defies description. The best I can do is compare it to raw onion juice boiled in hell. The only word in the English language that can describe such a wretched odor is the one most often used by children: Pee-YEW!

And that's what was coming up through the floor and invading every corner of our happy little home. The skunk wasn't in the garage this time, or in the yard. He was under the house.

Have you ever wondered what you would do if you had a skunk under your house? It's a very interesting problem. What makes it especially interesting is that there are four or five solutions, and any one of them can prove worse than the problem itself.

I once heard the story about an elderly lady who lived on a farm in the Texas Panhandle. Four skunks took up residence under her house and the smell became unbearable. She asked her son to do something about it, but he was busy with the field work and didn't get around to it.

One night the dear lady decided she had had enough. She couldn't stand another minute of it and she intended to do something about it. She loaded up her shotgun and fetched a flashlight. Holding the light in one hand and the gun in the other, she blasted all four skunks and some of the plumbing.

She solved the immediate problem but she also had to abandon the house and move in with her son. And the son was left with the hellish dilemma of how to get four dead skunks out from under the house. Boy, I wish I'd been there to hear what he said when he crawled out.

Well, I didn't shoot our skunk. I thought about poison but decided against that too. Where do you suppose a poisoned skunk would go to die? Under the house.

It finally occurred to me that in this age of scientific wonders, there still isn't a good solution to a polecat under the house. It's a little bit like being married. Sometimes the other party makes you so mad you want to wring her neck, but if you even raise your voice, you're going to catch hell. That ain't even hardly a fair fight.

74

Country Roads

John Denver sings a song called "Country Road." In the song, he asks the road to take him back to the place where he grew up and belongs. It's a nice song. It must have been a nice road too, because it made John Denver rich.

I got to thinking about that yesterday as I rumbled over one of the thirteen cattleguards that stand between us and the little town of Beaver, Oklahoma, which we sometimes call Civilization.

John Denver's song is so sweet and nice (I said to myself), I'm inclined to think that he does most of his driving on pavement.

If he drove our country road for about two weeks, I think he would change his tune, and probably some of the words. Whatever song he managed to compose about our road couldn't be sung in the presence of ladies and children, since it would almost certainly contain naughty language.

Now, you take those thirteen cattleguards as an example. A cattleguard is a wonderful invention. It spares you the time and effort of opening and closing a pasture gate. Heck of a good idea. When it is properly set and leveled, you can zip right over it without losing much speed.

But when it's not properly set and leveled, and when you don't know it, you sometimes get a nasty surprise.

Last Saturday an oil company sent one of those giant carry-alls down into our country to dredge out some caliche and distribute it on several slick spots in the road. That was a noble idea, in spite of all the fifty pound boulders they left in the middle of the road.

But what effect do you suppose a loaded carry-all had on our little cattleguards? It mashed them into the ground. The cattleguards are now four inches lower than the road. The trip to town used to take thirty minutes. Now it takes anywhere from an hour to two days, depending on how fast you hit the first cattleguard, the extent of the damage, and how long it takes the wrecker to make it out from town.

We also look forward to the times when drilling contractors move rigs into the neighborhood. For some reason, this always seems to occur right after a rain. By the time the trucks and bulldozers have finished cutting up the road, you need either a half-track or a long-legged horse to make it through the ruts.

It is my misfortune to be the owner of two small cars, of the variety often referred to as "economy" cars. I have discovered that the term "economy" applies to gas mileage and not to maintenance. My cars get about twenty-six miles to a gallon of gas. On these country roads, I get about the same mileage on a front end job, and slightly better on a set of tires.

I own small cars because, the ratio of cowboy wages to car prices being what it is, our relationship has taken on the character of " 'til death do us part."

There is a humorous side to this fate of driving tincan automobiles over pasture roads, and I suppose it is apparent to the citizens of Beaver every time we drive into town.

When we take the Pinto, I'm sure we look and sound like the Grapes of Wrath. We have no hub caps on the left side, since we have planted both of them somewhere in Stanley

77

Barby's river pasture. The left front wheel is crooked and the front end on the left side sags lower than the right, dating back to the day in January when my wife plowed through mud and snow and discovered too late that the county crew had reset the third cattleguard and had left it three inches higher than the road.

She landed somewhere on the other side, with one child in her lap and the other under the back seat. She told me later that she had heard an awful crunch of metal.

I told her not to worry, that most likely she had merely broken a spring or a shock. I was later informed by a mechanic that the frame was merely bent.

And there is the little matter of muffler noise on the Pinto. We dragged the muffler across mud and snow and sand for many months before the exhaust pipe finally broke off at the manifold. I wired it up with baling wire, until I could "get around to fixing it," as we say in this business.

Nowadays, when we go roaring down the streets of Beaver in an attempt to make it to church on time, all the teenage hot-rodders look at us and wave and honk their horns. That is a trifle embarrassing to a grown man with two small children in the car.

The Vega is in better shape, though its gradual disintegration is proceeding at an orderly pace. We haven't dragged the muffler off the Vega yet, but we have managed to crack the exhaust manifold, so that the motor has the sound of emphysema.

About a month ago the county maintainer came by and smoothed up the road and threw some choice boulders up in the middle. We are accustomed to dodging boulders, but one evening I hit one a good square lick in the Vega. It produced a horrible squeal in the motor. Friends who know more about these things than I do have told me that the rock bent the flywheel housing. All I know is that it makes a hellacious noise.

When we drive the Vega down the street in Beaver, the hot-rodders don't honk and wave. They stare and then burst into gales of laughter.

I'm sure all of this is very funny to the people who see our poor battered cars as they wheeze and squeal through town. If we had a couple of hens roosting on the back seat, our image as Ma and Pa Kettle would be complete.

John Denver's country road made him rich. Mine is making me a clown and a pauper. Something is wrong here, and I think there is a lesson to be learned.

If a guy has to get involved with a country road, he'd be a whole lot better off if he figured out how to sing about it instead of drive over it.

Musskeeters

The other day I was out prowling pastures on horseback. It was getting toward noon and I started feeling a little gant, so I rode down to the creek where I knew there was a thicket of nice fat sandhill plums.

I got down and was in the process of cutting a swath through the plums when I heard a man's voice. It sounded like he was talking to someone. I crept a little closer and peered through the bushes.

There sat an old cowboy named Joe, who worked on a neighboring ranch. He was sitting with his back against a big cottonwood tree. In one hand he held a baloney sandwich, and in the other a thermos of coffee. His paint horse was tied to a bush nearby, grazing on the tall grass in the creek bottom. Joe must have been looking for strays that morning and stopped for dinner on the creek.

As I say, he was talking to himself. I didn't want to embarrass him, so I just squatted down and listened.

"Lord," he said, holding up his sandwich, "I want to thank you for the grub. It ain't much, but I'm proud to have it just the same. It'll keep my belly button from rubbin' up agin my backbone for a while."

81

He took a bite out of the sandwich, swigged on the thermos, and continued.

"Now Lord, there's a couple more things I want to take up with you while they're fresh on my mind. You sent us some fine rain this spring. I dug a few postholes last week, and by crackies, we've got subsoil moisture for the first time in five years. And I don't know when I've seen better grass at this time of the year. I want you to know that I'm thankful for it.

"But Lord, dadgum it, did you have to send all these gnats and musskeeters too?" At that very moment, he swatted a mosquito on his arm. "There, you see that? He was drillin' right through my shirt. I don't want to complain, but it just don't seem fair to me. For five years we suffered with the heat and the dirt and the wind. For five years we watched the clouds bank up in the east and rain on someone else. Now you send us rain and grass and wild flowers and fresh air. You've put Sunday clothes on this hard old country, and a man just naturally wants to get on his horse and ride through it.

"But how can a man enjoy your creation when the dadgum bugs carry him off his horse? They've punched holes in me from the tops of my boots to the sweatband of my hat. I've got musskeeter bites in places I couldn't talk about in polite company. I can't hardly sit still a minute for scratchin'. And what the musskeeters haven't chewed up, the gnats are buzzin' over. I never seen the like of bugs."

He took another bite of the sandwich. "Now I've thought about this all day, so what I'm about to say ain't comin' off the top of my hat. I know you're a good deal smarter than this old cowboy, but I think that on this business of bugs you can stand a little correctin'.

"In the first place, it ain't fair to make us pay for moisture with the hide off our backs. If you're gonna pretty up this country, then you ought to let us enjoy it. Otherwise, you might as well leave it dry and ugly. The way it is now, the only people who can enjoy it are the confounded bugs.

"In the second place, I don't appreciate that I have to feed *your* bugs. In this country, we try to live by the rules. If a man runs cattle, he keeps up his fences and keeps his stock at home. If a man owns a bunch of dogs, he's got to buy the feed for them. Now, I don't mind feedin' a man's dog once in a while, and you won't hear me complain if the neighbor's steers come through the fence now and then.

"But Lord, for cryin' out loud, I've been feedin' your musskeeters all summer long! And to tell you the truth, I feel like I've been over-grazed. If you're smart enough to make a musskeeter in the first place, a little bitty thing that can swoop and fly and buzz and bite and find me no matter where I am in the pasture—if you're smart enough to make that little piece of machinery that never needs grease or oil or gas or STP, then you're smart enough to figger out how to feed him yourself.

"If we're gonna be neighbors in this old world, you're gonna have to do something about your bugs. I've pastured a good herd of them all summer long and I don't want no more. You made 'em, you feed 'em. I don't know what kind of fence it'll take to keep them bugs at home, but I wish you'd start lookin' into it right now.

"If you ask me, you ought to send every last one of 'em to hell and throw up a good stout fence to keep 'em there. If you can't do that, then why don't you learn 'em to eat on your preachers and to leave us cowboys alone."

Joe squinted his eyes and waved a finger toward the sky. And he raised his voice.

"Now Lord, I've never been the kind of man who made threats, but I've had about a bellyful of your gnats and musskeeters. If them bugs keep chewin' on me, I'm gonna take action against you. Every time I get bit, I'm gonna curse and swear. I'm gonna use more chewing tobacker than ever. I'm gonna buy me a bottle of whiskey. I'm gonna stop going to church once a month. I'm gonna be mean to little children. I'm gonna kick my horse once a day, and whip my dog too. I'm gonna . . .

A line of thunderhead clouds had moved overhead by this

time, and all at once a bolt of lightning came crashing down out of the sky. It struck the cottonwood tree and cut it half in two. This was followed by an ear-splitting boom.

Joe dropped his sandwich, rolled into a ball, and covered up his head. When the limbs and leaves had stopped falling, he crawled out from under his hat and looked up toward the sky. Then he picked up the sandwich, dusted off the grass, and took another bite.

"Well, Lord," he said in a shakey voice, "like I was sayin', thanks for the baloney and the moisture. And we sure have been enjoyin' them musskeeters you sent. Amen."

Weather Mortification

The other day I was out to the vet's with a lame horse. The vet looked him over and said the trouble was a cracked hoof up front. It had split up to the quick and gotten infected.

"Well," I asked the vet, "can you give him a shot to take care of the problem?" He gave me a pair of hoof nippers and a good cussing. I always did say that vet was a smart aleck. When I want a prescription for myself, I'll go to a doctor.

While I was out there, old Charlie came in and we got to talking. He'd got a little shower the night before. The gauge showed fifteen hunderts, but there was a spider in the bottom of the glass. It took us about ten minutes to decide that the weather was hot and dry.

"Say," Charlie piped up, "what do you think about all this weather mortification business?"

I pulled on my chin and squinted one eye. "Well, the way I get it, some people think it's all right. But on the other hand, you've got quite a bunch that thinks it's not so good. Then there's the ones in the middle who haven't quite made up their minds."

He nodded. "That's the way it looks to me too. But what do you think about it?"

"Well, I agree with 'em, Charlie."

"You do?"

"Up to a point."

He said that's the way he felt about it too. He bought a box of sulfa boluses and left.

I didn't give old Charlie a straight answer on weather mortification because I didn't want to get into a fuss with him. But I do have some opinions about it.

G. L. Holmes

In the first place, I don't want the wheat farmers in charge of mortifying the weather. They want rain in the fall to get up their wheat, but my grass doesn't grow in the fall and I don't want the cured grass washed away. Can't use a rain in October.

But I sure could use a nice soaking rain around the middle of June to give the buffalo and grama a kick, but that's just the time when the wheat farmers are trying to get the grain out of the fields. So as long as cowmen are in charge of changing the weather, I'm all for making it rain.

In the second place, if they're going to set up one of those silver bromide generators on my place, I want to be sure I get all the rain that comes from it. I don't want those seeded clouds drifting up to Kansas or down into Texas. That happens enough the way it is.

And I don't want my neighbors getting any of it either. I get along with my neighbors, but there's nothing in the world that makes me feel better than to tell the fellow on the next ranch that I got an inch of rain when he only got twenty hunderts. Hearing him cuss at times like that is sweeter than music.

When you beat your neighbors on rainfall, you know you're a better manager than they are.

And in the third place, as long as we're going to fiddle with the weather, we might as well go all the way. I've got plenty of gripes about this weather, and I'd like to get something done about them.

You take the matter of snow. All the kids love it, but they don't have to fool with tire chains when it's twenty above zero, and they don't have to feed hay to a bunch of hungry cows.

I think snow's pretty on Christmas day, and there's where we ought to keep it. I vote we abolish snow except on Christmas.

And while I'm complaining about the weather, I'll go on to say that our winters are too danged cold and the summers are too danged hot. We've got too danged much wind in the spring and too danged much calm in the fall.

A man can't get any work done in the winter for the cold, and in the summer it's just too hot. In the spring, you can't get anything done for all that blasted wind, and in the fall—well, that's football season, and it's too pretty to work anyway. That leaves about three days a year for the ranch work, and that's one reason some of us don't get out horses trimmed up. It's all because of the weather.

So there's my ideas on weather mortification. I want rain when I want it, but not when I don't. I want rain on my place, but not on the neighbor's. I want the summers cold and the winters hot, except for Christmas day, and then I'll take three inches of snow if it'll melt off by the middle of the afternoon.

And I want to move the March wind over into August so I won't have to haul water in dog days.

I think that just about covers it. No, one more thing. I'd like to change the weather, but not so much that we won't have anything to complain about. In these parts, if we stopped complaining about the weather, there would be a powerful lot of silence.

Cowboy Museum

About a year ago the citizens of our country decided it was time to start preserving their pioneer heritage, so they had a bake sale and a couple of bingo parties, raised some money, and founded the Pioneer and Cowboy Museum.

They asked people in the area to donate stuff. When they got to me, I had to tell them that all my antiques were in service, and that if somebody didn't slow down inflation, I was liable to have a little museum of my own in about five years.

Willie, my neighbor, wasn't too impressed with the museum. We went through it together one afternoon. When we got outside, he rolled a hot tamale and gave his opinion: "It ain't akrit."

"I thought they did a pretty fair job myself," I said.

"Nope. They got it all wrong." He put the torch to his smoke. "They've got all that junk in there, but I didn't see the one thing that's kept ranches going all these years. It's the cowboy's most important piece of equipment, and they don't have it in their moozim. It ain't akrit."

"Well now, hold on," I said. "They've got spurs and saddles and chaps and bits and guns and a chuckwagon. And they have that stuffed horse."

"I thought that was a dinosaur."

"No, it was a stuffed horse."

Willie shrugged. "That's too bad. I thought the dinosaur was the best part."

"What's this piece of equipment you're talking about?"

He slit his eyes at me. "You really don't know?"

"No, I thought they had everything, and until you prove me wrong, I'm going to say it's a nice little museum."

He grunted. "The six-gun may have won the West. Spurs may have kept the ponies moving up the trail. Saddles may have kept a few punchers off the ground. That's all real nice, but the thing that's kept this whole country from falling apart," he drilled me in the chest with his finger, "is baling wire, and I didn't see one piece of it in that so-called museum."

I lifted my hat and scratched my head. "Oh."

"If that museum had been real and true to life, they would have had bundles of baling wire all over the place so you could stumble over it. They would have it hanging on every board and peg in the place.

"Their head stalls should have been patched with it, and the curb straps should have been made of it. All them spurs should have had heel straps made of baling wire. And look at that front door. It's got store-boughten hinges and a new lock. Any cowboy worth shootin' would have had that door hard-wared up with good wire."

"Well," I said, "you've got a point, Willie, but I think you're beating it to death."

"Nope. Fact is fact. The reason we won this country from the Indians is because we had baling wire and they didn't. If them pioneers hadn't had baling wire, their houses would have fallen down the first year, they wouldn't have had any rigging to put on a horse, and there wouldn't be a bob wire fence or a set of corrals standing in the country today.

"If I was running that museum, I'd throw out all that Hollywood junk—and that stuffed donkey with it—and fill up

90

every room with good baling wire. That would tell the whole story."

"It might tell the whole story," I said, "but who would come to see it? You have to admit that a building full of baling wire would be a little dull."

Willie made a sour face and nodded. "I know, I thought of that. But that's the whole trouble with telling the truth. It tends to get awful danged teejus."

Big Night on the Town

We live on a ranch, way out in the country. We don't go to town much because it's too much trouble. But now and then we crave some excitement. It usually starts like this:

It's ten o'clock at night. The kids are finally in bed and the house is quiet. You and the wife split a Dr. Pepper and sit down in the living room.

She looks at you. "How long has it been since we went anywhere?" You scratch your chin and start to answer, then she adds, "Grocery shopping and church don't count."

"Well, let's see. We went to town back in June."

She raises one brow. "Dear, that was to get a wheel bearing for the stock trailer. That doesn't count either. When was the last time we went to a movie?"

"Oh, a movie. Hmm." There is a long silence.

"See?" she says. "You can't even remember. Well, I have a wonderful idea. Tomorrow night, let's take the kids to a babysitter and go to a movie."

You yawn. "Why tomorrow night?"

"It's my birthday, you clod."

"Your birthday? I thought your birthday was in August."

"This IS August."

"Oh. I guess it is." You shake your head and wonder where the time has gone. "What's showing?"

"I don't know, but let's go and find out. We both need a night out. It'll be fun."

"All right, that's a good idea," you say. "I've got an easy day tomorrow. I'm just going to ride pastures and check the cattle. I should be back early." You give her a smile. "We'll just go to a movie and have a big night out. If I remember right, tomorrow's your birthday."

She throws a magazine at you.

The next morning you have your day planned out so that you'll be back at the house by four o'clock. That will give you plenty of time for evening chores, supper, and a bath. You hook up the stock trailer, load your horse, and head for the first pasture.

The windmill isn't making water. It pumped all summer and never missed a lick, but today, since you want to quit early, the leathers decided to wear out. Do you fix it now or leave it until tomorrow—and dream all night about cattle dying of thirst?

Better go ahead and pull it, but you won't take the time to go back to the house for ropes and pulleys. The well is only seventy-five feet deep. You can pull it by hand.

When the leathers come out of the cylinder, they turn backward. For half an hour you strain and sweat and grunt. You turn blue in the face and your arms feel as though they're going to fall off. Then ten feet from the top, it stops. You get the last rod out with a high-lift jack.

By the time you get everything hooked up and running again, you're an hour behind schedule.

You skip lunch and go on to the other pastures. You have to rope and doctor one calf for pinkeye, but everything else is all right. It's three o'clock and you have one pasture left. If you hurry, you'll make it home by 4:30 or 5:00.

You lope through the pasture and get your count—all but

one cow. You know which one is missing, that little bald-face cow with the snub horns. The last time you saw her, she was quite pregnant. She's off somewhere having a calf. You know she's had the calf. You know she's all right. But you've got to check to make sure.

You start around the pasture in a high lope. You check all the water holes, plum thickets, and shade trees. She ain't there. The old fool. She went to the backest part of the back side of the pasture.

In anger, you jab the spurs into your pony. Startled, he comes within one jump of planting you in a sandhill.

You head for the back side and, yep, there she is, grazing beside her new calf. But you had to check.

It's 4:30 and you're still running an hour behind. You start back to the house. On the road, you meet your neighbor.

Now, old Charlie is the best neighbor in the world, a prince of a guy. But damn him, he'll talk your ear off. If you're in a hurry, you want to avoid Charlie.

You look for a feed road to turn on. Nope. Well, maybe you can slip by and he won't recognize you. Nope. He pulls over to the side of the road and stops, rolls down his window and sticks his grinning face out to greet you.

Charlie covers the usual topics. Grass is getting awful short. Sure need some moisture. Flies is bad. Pickup hasn't been running right. Okra just hasn't done much this year. The Arnolds' milk cow had twins. Lonnie Stewart ran a skunk through his new swather. That bay horse, the one that Pete Moses used to ride, got cut up in barbed wire.

You drum your fingers on the steering wheel and wait for Charlie to run out of wind. Finally, when he stops to sneeze, you jump in.

"Well, Charlie, guess I'd better get along." It's five o'clock. You go roaring down the road, fly over the last three cattle guards, and park beside the barn.

You're home, but you're not through.

94

You unsaddle your horse, water him, give him grain, and turn him out to pasture. You mix up a bottle of milk replacer and hurry to feed the orphan calf. The little snot has scours. You run to the house to get two raw eggs. Your wife meets you at the door.

"Have you forgotten that we're going to the show tonight?"

Your eyes turn red, smoke coils out of your nostrils, and you are about to bellow like a wounded bull. But this isn't the time for a fight. She doesn't understand, so you tell her that you're hurrying as fast as you can.

You run back to the barn, mix the raw eggs into the milk, and trot to the calf pen. The calf takes the nipple and rolls it around in his mouth. He doesn't know whether he likes eggs in his milk or not.

"Will you eat and stop fooling around!" Finally, he takes hold and drinks it down.

You wash the bottle and nipple, close up the saddle room, close up the barn, unhook the stock trailer, park the pickup in the shed, and close the door.

At last, you're done.

You skip supper. (You skipped lunch too, and your belly is growling like a panther.) You hurry through your shave. (Three little balls of toilet paper check the bleeding while you jump into your clothes.)

No one talks on the way to town. At eighty miles an hour, everybody's thoughts have turned to eternity. It's 7:20 when you leave the babysitter's house, turn onto Main Street, and head for the theater.

At last, you begin to relax. "Well, we'll miss the first part of the show, but we'll see some of it."

You park in front of the theater and look up at the marquee to see what's showing. You curse and slap your forehead with the palm of your hand. Your wife groans aloud and mutters, "I don't believe it."

You have spent all day running in circles. You haven't eaten since breakfast. You almost cut your throat shaving. You had to spank the kids three times.

And the movie is called . . . GANG RAPE.

You sit in silence. Then your wife says, "Well, do you need to pick up a wheel bearing or something?"

"I've got a better idea. Let's get an ice cream cone."

"That sounds nice."

"Happy Birthday, dear."

You get the ice cream cone, drag Main Street three times, pick up the kids, and head back to the ranch.

Well, you got it out of your system. Now you're ready to stay home for another six months.

Colts and Little Boys

In my dual capacity as ranch manager and father, I have noticed a phenomenon which is nowhere mentioned either by Dr. Spock or in my copy of *The Stockman's Handbook*: there are certain similarities between young horses and little boys.

The occasion for this observation arose when, in July, 1975, one of the mares on the ranch gave birth to a filly foal which we called Calipso. At that same time, my wife and I had a son named Scottie who had just passed the yearling mark.

As nearly as I can tell, the young of both species are preserved, not on the strength of their present behavior, but on the ancient hope that some day they will amount to something.

In the case of the colt, you hope that eventually he will be broke to ride, trained, and taught to carry out the duties of a ranch horse. In the case of a little boy, you hope that in time he will display what, for lack of a better term, parents often refer to as "civilized behavior."

In both cases the hope often exceeds the evidence that things will actually turn out that way.

When Calipso reached the age of six months, I weaned her off her mother's milk, placed her in a pen by herself, and made my first attempts at establishing a friendly relationship with her. Her response to this was to dash around the pen, foil my attempts at putting a halter on her head, and cringe, wince, and quiver at the touch of my hand.

She was as wild as a jackrabbit, and at that point the possibility that she would ever submit to discipline and training seemed as remote as the stars.

I confined her to a small pen and began rubbing and petting her to win her confidence. On Christmas Eve of 1975, I was in the pen with her, stroking her hindquarters and talking softly. She still cringed at my touch, but had ceased throwing herself around the pen. On this particular evening, when Santa Claus was loading his sleigh at the North Pole, I noticed that Calipso was hopping up and down on her front legs when I touched her. I was wondering what this might mean when she let me know, by kicking me squarely in the groin.

The agonies that followed need not be enumerated. Some forms of education are more painful than others.

The months of training stretched into a year, then a year and a half. In July, 1977, I took Calipso out into the pasture for our first solo ride. She seemed to be doing very well. We rode for half an hour through the sandhills in the middle pasture, and though she was green and awkward, she did not try to buck.

This pleased me, since you rather expect a little rodeo action the first time out. I began to relax and enjoy the ride, at which time she dropped her head between her legs, broke in half, and did a respectable imitation of what goes on at the National Finals Rodeo. After three jumps, she had me sprawled across her neck, and on the fourth she bedded me down in a clump of sagebrush.

But then came the day when Calipso changed from a colt into a saddle mare, the day when she finally understood what she was supposed to do. Instead of flinching at grasshoppers and balking at every shadow, she pranced out with the proud

98

carriage of her Arabian forebears. When I pulled back the rein, she stopped. When I told her to get up, she moved.

All at once, we were no longer two warring creatures, but one flesh and one will, wedded together into a mighty centaur. In spite of herself, Calipso had become a ranch horse.

The most obvious point of similarity between colts and little boys is that both resist the civilizing influence of their keepers. Scottie, like Calipso, went through a wild-as-a-jackrabbit stage.

I recall one night in particular. I was babysitting while my wife attended a club meeting in town. During the meal, Scottie turned his milk glass upside-down on the table. While I was in the kitchen trying to find a towel, he dumped a plate of food on the floor and dirtied his pants. As I recall, he was more amused by these antics than I.

Then there was the time, early in his second year, when he discovered that he could crawl across the cattleguard in front of the house, and he began wandering off in a pasture that contained 2,500 acres under one fence (that's four square miles.)

Parents who don't believe in spanking children have probably never had to worry about their children being eaten by coyotes. We worried, and we spanked.

Like Calipso, Scottie grew and developed. His little mind began to show intelligence and curiosity, and I began taking him with me in the pickup when I went out to feed cattle, check windmills, and mend fence.

But intelligence can be a mixed blessing. We thought it cute when he imitated Daddy by "checking cattle" in the living room and wearing my cowboy hat around the house. But then came the day when he snitched a plug of Daddy's chewing tobacco and gave it a try, and the day he stunned Grandmother Erickson with a sample of barnyard language. I still don't know where he learned it.

And like Calipso, Scottie passed through a rebellious pe-

99

riod when we resigned ourselves to the fact that he would become a criminal or an outcast, and that all our efforts at civilizing him had come to nothing. This was shortly after his third birthday. He seemed to take fiendish delight in making little girls cry and dragging our poor cat around the porch by her tail. He began referring to his elders as "dummy," and once responded to his grandmother's command by spitting at her.

He learned something important about grandmothers on that occasion: if provoked, they can be dangerous.

But, as in the case of the colt, there came a time when we suddenly realized that Scottie had left his babyhood forever and had become a boy. All at once his pants were striking him several inches above the ankles, his boots could hardly contain his feet any longer, and the baby fat disappeared from his face. Whereas before, his primary form of communication had been a two-letter word (no), he began saying "yes" and "please" and "thank you" and "may I."

And he said his prayers at night ("God bless Uncle Scot and Auntie Lawren and Uncle Scot's boat.") And kissing his mother and father good night became his own idea. And best of all, he stopped spitting.

Looking back on things, I wonder if I was prepared to cope with the double-barrel action of a colt and a little boy. I suspect not, but I doubt that anyone ever is. Raising colts and little boys is one of those things for which there is no adequate preparation. You fall into it through ignorance, live to regret it, and suddenly realize one day that the experience has left you with some of the most cherished memories of your life.

For that alone, the human race will continue to break horses and raise children.

John R. Erickson is the author of 19 books and hundreds of articles. His work has appeared in the *Dallas Times Herald, Texas Highways, Western Horseman, Persimmon Hill, The Cattleman, Livestock Weekly,* and many other places. He is a member of the Texas Institute of Letters, the Philosophical Society of Texas and the Western Writers of America. He lives in Perryton, Texas, with his wife Kristine and their three children.

Drawings by Gerald L. Holmes have appeared in *Beef Magazine, Western Horseman, The Cattleman,* and other places. He has published one book of cartoons, *Pickens County,* and his work has illustrated 12 of John Erickson's books. He and his wife Carol live in Perryton with their two sons.

Printed by Cushing-Malloy, Inc., Ann Arbor, Michigan.

Designed and produced by *Innovative Publishing*, P. O. Box 580, Perryton, Texas, 79070.

MORE GREAT ENTERTAINMENT
BY JOHN R. ERICKSON

ACE REID: COWPOKE

Ace Reid: Cowpoke by John R. Erickson. Photographs and cartoons. Index. Clothbound $15.95.

This biography is a milestone in western writing, for it brings together two of the most popular humorists of our day: Ace Reid and John Erickson. When these two cowboys get together, the result is a book you won't be able to put down.

The HANK THE COWDOG Series of Books
by John R. Erickson
Drawings by Gerald L. Holmes

Hank the Cowdog

The Further Adventures of Hank the Cowdog

It's a Dog's Life

Murder in the Middle Pasture

Faded Love

Let Sleeping Dogs Lie

The Curse of the Incredible Priceless Corncob

The Case of the One-eyed Killer Stud Horse

Paperbacks $5.95 each   Hardbacks $9.95 each

JOHN R. ERICKSON'S
STORIES ON CASSETTE TAPE

Each two cassette tapeset features Erickson reading all the parts in character, plus songs, background music and sound effects.

Hank the Cowdog

The Further Adventures of Hank the Cowdog

It's a Dog's Life

Murder in the Middle Pasture

Faded Love

Let Sleeping Dogs Lie

The Curse of the Incredible Priceless Corncob

The Case of the One-eyed Killer Stud Horse

The Devil in Texas and Other Cowboy Tales

TAPESETS $13.95 each

Hank the Cowdog's Greatest Hits

Single tape $6.95

MORE GREAT BOOKS
BY JOHN R. ERICKSON

Cowboy Country. Photographs by Kris Erickson. Hardback $13.95.

The Modern Cowboy. Photographs by Kris Erickson. Paperback $6.95.

Panhandle Cowboy. Photographs by Bill Ellzey. Paperback $5.95.

The Hunter. (Historical novel) Hardback $9.95.

Essays on Writing and Publishing. (How-to book) Paperback $5.00.

COWBOY HUMOR
BY JOHN R. ERICKSON

Cowboys Are a Separate Species

Cowboys Are Partly Human

Alkali County Tales or If at First You Don't Succeed, Get a Bigger Hammer

The Devil in Texas and Other Cowboy Tales

Paperbacks $5.95 each   Hardbacks $9.95 each

Cowboys Are a Separate Species

Alkali County Tales

Cowboys Are Partly Human

The Devil in Texas

MAVERICK BOOKS ORDER FORM

Name _____

Address _____

City _____ State _____ Zip _____

Visa/MasterCard _____ Expires _____

Visa or MasterCard orders may call 1-800-722-HANK
in Texas call 1-(806) 435-7611 . Please have your card at hand.

Description	Price	Quantity	Total

*Texas residents include **6 1/4 %**
 (.0625)

Subtotal _____

**If subtotal is:

Sales Tax* _____

less than $14.00	add $1.50
$14.01 to $20.00	add $2.00
$20.01 to $30.00	add $2.75
$30.01 to $40.00	add $3.50
over $40.00	add $4.00

Postage** _____
 and handling

Total _____

Maverick Books, Inc. Box 549, Perryton, Texas 79070 / (806) 435-7611
Please feel free to reproduce this form.

MAVERICK BOOKS ORDER FORM

Name _____

Address _____

City _____ State _____ Zip _____

Visa/MasterCard _____ Expires _____

**Visa or MasterCard orders may call 1-800-722-HANK
in Texas call 1-(806) 435-7611 . Please have your card at hand.**

Description	Price	Quantity	Total

*Texas residents include **6 1/4 %**
(.0625)

Subtotal _____

**If subtotal is:

Sales Tax* _____

less than $14.00	add $1.50
$14.01 to $20.00	add $2.00
$20.01 to $30.00	add $2.75
$30.01 to $40.00	add $3.50
over $40.00	add $4.00

Postage** _____
  and handling

Total _____

Maverick Books, Inc. Box 549, Perryton, Texas 79070 / (806) 435-7611
Please feel free to reproduce this form.

MAVERICK BOOKS ORDER FORM

Name _____

Address _____

City _____ State _____ Zip _____

Visa/MasterCard _____ Expires _____

Visa or MasterCard orders may call 1-800-722-HANK
in Texas call 1-(806) 435-7611 . Please have your card at hand.

Description	Price	Quantity	Total

*Texas residents include **6 1/4 %**
(.0625)   Subtotal _____

**If subtotal is: Sales Tax* _____
  less than $14.00   add $1.50
  $14.01 to $20.00   add $2.00   Postage** _____
  $20.01 to $30.00   add $2.75   and handling
  $30.01 to $40.00   add $3.50
  over $40.00   add $4.00   Total _____

Maverick Books, Inc. Box 549, Perryton, Texas 79070 / (806) 435-7611
Please feel free to reproduce this form.